St. Benedict's Rule for Business Success

St. Benedict's Rule
for
Business Success

QUENTIN R. SKRABEC, JR.

Purdue University Press
West Lafayette, Indiana

Printed in the United States of America

Library of Congress Cataloging-in-Publication Data

Skrabec, Quentin R.
    St. Benedict's rule for business success / Quentin R. Skrabec, Jr.
        p. cm.
    Includes bibliographical references
    ISBN 1-55753-254-0 (cloth : alk. paper)
        1. Business—Religious aspects—Christianity.
2. Benedictines—Rules. I. Title: Saint Benedict's rule for business
success. II. Benedict, Saint, Abbot of Monte Cassino. Regula.
III. Title.

    HF5388 .S554 2002
    650—dc21

                                                        2002141449

To the women who have made this book possible—
my mother, Dori, and the Blessed Mother Mary

Contents

Preface

In addition to the professed monastics who follow the Benedictine way of life, however, there are innumerable lay-persons around the globe who also find the rule a guide and a ground rule for their own lives in the middle of a chaotic and challenging world.

—Joan D. Chittister, *The Rule of Benedict*

For the man of the twentieth century, root-less and isolated, sure a vision may need transformation before it can be made real, but its appeal is undeniable.

—Anthony C. Meisel and M. L. del Mastro, *The Rule of Saint Benedict*

The Rule of Saint Benedict has been con-sidered as important as the constitution of any temporal state, and all of literature, it has been said, it was second to the bible in its influence.

—James Joseph Rorimer, *The Cloisters*

Benedict's Rule incorporates the teaching of many other monastic and ecclesiastical sources. Like all monastic Rules, the Rule of Benedict is not a spiritual or theological treatise, but rather a compendium of practical directives, a concretization of Scripture as a guide for daily life.

—Elizabeth M. Hallam, *Saints*

[The Rule] is the spirituality of the twenty-first century because it deals with issues facing us now—stewardship, relationships, authority, community, balance, work, simplicity, prayer and spiritual and psychological development.

—Joan D. Chittister, *The Rule of Benedict*

As a manufacturing manager and quality engineer, I have always stood in awe of the product and service excellence of monasteries. Their cathedrals, art, printing, manufacturing, and learning embodied the very meaning of human excellence. Their quality surpassed their historical mentors of Greece and Rome. What, I have often asked myself, enabled this to happen?

This question was more than just idle speculation to me. In the 1970s and 1980s I was part of the American manufacturing community's search for excellence. We were being badly beaten in the marketplace by the Japanese, and Japanese techniques thus seemed to be the answer to our own problems. America thus adopted, adjusted, and dictated the use of such Japanese techniques as team manning, employee empowerment, consensus, kaizen, and statistical process control. But the implementation of the Japanese versions of these techniques met with much resistance, and culturally there were issues that prevented a full implementation of Japanese-style teams. Japanese team implementation resulted in the erosion and loss of our traditional strength of the individual. Yet I pushed on (as did most of American businesses), even becoming highly successful at "adapting" the Japanese "team." One "adaptation" led my team to the first National Quality Cup for Teams by *USA Today,* landing us on the cover. Like most middle managers, however, I knew that despite their success these were not true Japanese teams but rather were Western versions of the original. To satisfy the belief of upper management that success was in the Japanese style, this knowledge remained our secret. A true model was lacking for this Western version which achieved success.

What became obvious to me was that to succeed the Western version needed to leave room for a blend of individual performance with the concept of team goals, and not simply be based on the idea of a consensus-based non-individualistic approach.

Furthermore, implementation of Japanese process controls was not, in reality, changing business. Our major industries were still failing at an alarming rate. As a boy from Pittsburgh, I was in awe of the great steel complexes of the valleys. Andrew Carnegie was a Pittsburgh god of sorts. The steel industry had been the heart of my family for generations. As a baby boomer, I had seen it reach its zenith of power. As a young metallurgist, I entered the industry of my boyhood dreams in the 1970s. Like St. Benedict with the Roman Empire (of his love), I was born too late. I was to see the fall of steel and many great American industries. I really felt like Benedict feeling grief, dismay, sadness, and frustration. As had happened to Rome, the barbarians came and leveled the great mills of Pittsburgh, Cleveland, Youngstown, and Chicago. I was quality manager of the Jones and Laughlin mill in Pittsburgh. At its peak, it employed 22,000 and covered miles of riverfront. That mill had made iron continuously for more than two hundred years. On its last day we had all the Japanese techniques and the much-heralded process control practices in place. I was to witness it torn down and sold for scrap. What was at the root of this failure?

Some 1,500 years ago, St. Benedict addressed the same questions as he studied the failure of Western culture propelled by the failure of Rome. He then drew on the great traditions, laws, and organization from his culture in order to build a new approach. Benedict's real contribution, however, was his analysis of what was needed to prevent the entropic decline of the Roman system. Rome had lacked a rule and discipline for its great system. Benedict proposed a new type of organizational Rule that was cybernetic. He had built in corrections to counter the natural tendency toward disorder of organizations (entropy). Furthermore, he built in a standard of excellence for human endeavors.

Benedict's techniques are pure fruits of Western culture. Benedict's concept of community is that of our sports teams, allowing an outlet for individual performance within the framework of team goals. As it is in sports teams, discipline is used in the Benedictine world to build team unity. Benedict's "teams" work within our political ideal of democracy and at the same time maximize employee involvement. Benedict clearly shows that consensus does not have an inherent advantage over democratic approaches. Benedict's concepts take employee empowerment to its ultimate—involvement in the selection of leaders. Unlike flat organizations that avoid addressing full employee involvement by downplaying leadership, Benedict's Rule reinforces the need for leadership.

Benedictine organizations feature a new approach to process control that offers results. Benedict finds the secret to excellence in building organization. Benedictine organizations are compatible with Western traditions of democracy, management, leadership, and organization, and can be the source of a new energy. The Benedictine approach does not require a revolution in organization—only a strengthening. Benedictine principles are not adaptations of military concepts or politics but original organizational designs.

Benedict was an organizational genius who worked in the field of organizational management. Benedict's organizational rules are timeless in application, having been in use for 1,500 years.

The *Rule of St. Benedict* is the oldest living organizational document in the Western world. The Rule was written to bring order to the rapidly growing monastic communities of the period. The Rule was not a spiritual guide, but an organizational guide for spiritual communities. It focused on procedures, hierarchy, and organization from a foundation of basic Christian principles. Yet much has been written on the compatibility of the Rule with all religions, especially Zen, Judaism, Taoism, and Hinduism. The Rule's strength, however, is in its basic pragmatic approach for any culture. A review of the seventy-three chapter headings (see appendix) shows the organizational detail of the Rule. The last fifty-two of the seventy-three chapters are totally dedicated to management and organization.

Translations of the Rule could fill a major city library. It is an amazing piece of Western civilization. It is the oldest functioning organizational constitution in existence. Even today, the more than 50,000 followers of Benedict are governed by the Rule. The Rule, however, is a timeless guide that has changed Western organizations over its 1,500 years of application.

Pope Gregory the Great used it in the late sixth century to reorganize the Catholic church's structure and hierarchy. That structure remains today and is the source of the simple seven layers of hierarchy used to govern the oldest and largest organization in the world. Charlemagne further demonstrated its broad application in the ninth century. Charlemagne applied the Rule to government and education, and through his unification of Europe spread its concepts throughout the West. The spread of the Rule not only brought order to the Dark Ages but also was the foundation of a new economic revolution.

In the Middle Ages, Benedictine organizations became the economic engines of Europe, organizing an agricultural world into a more technology-oriented society. Furthermore, the organizational structure of Benedictine monasteries allowed for the accumulation and use of information as never before.

The Rule today offers the same timeless insights for managers. The principles of employee empowerment, scientific management, and cooperative advantage are deeply rooted in the Rule. The basic organizational principles have found applications throughout history. For Western managers, the insights are culturally correct for our society because the Rule is part of Western civilization.

Introduction

The *Rule of St. Benedict* remains one of the most influential
and enduring documents of Western Civilization. The Rule
is believed to have been penned by Benedict of Nursia
around 530. Benedict was educated in Rome and had a
first-hand experience in the last days and fall of Roman society. Benedict had a great love for Roman law and order
but was horrified by its moral decay. From his experiences
with the fall of Rome, he developed a strong belief that law
and order required a strong moral community to have en-
durance. In 520, Benedict became a reformer of European
monasteries which were going the way of Rome. As part of
this reform movement, Benedict imposed an organizational
constitution which became known as the Rule of Benedict.

The first historical mention of the Rule is found in the
writings of Pope Gregory the Great (540–604). Gregory
hailed the rule for its "discretion and clarity of language."
Gregory the Great had lived under the Rule as a monk and
abbot at the monastery of St. Andrew in Rome. Gregory
used the Rule to organize the infrastructure of the church. By
his universal application of the Rule in the Church and government, Gregory built the foundation of the Holy Roman

Empire. Gregory's reform remains today in the church some 1,400 years later.

While we have many references to the Rule—including Gregory's writings on it—the original text has been lost. According to legend, the original text was destroyed in a fire at the Tecno monastery in 896. The earliest surviving text (known as Codex 914) can today be found in the monastic library of St. Gall in Switzerland, and dates to 900. It was from this text that Charlemagne commissioned a copy to be made for use across the Holy Roman Empire.

Translations of the Rule do exhibit some minor variations. Benedict wrote in a fifth century contemporary version of Latin which is less precise than classical Latin. This book is based on the 1975 translation by Anthony Meisel and M. L. del Mastro, available from Imoge Books (Doubleday) and containing additional translators' notes. This translation offers a full text instead of the many short versions that are also in circulation.

The text of the Rule itself is about sixty pages in normal typescript. It consists of seventy-three "chapters," which average from three to five paragraphs. A full listing of these chapter titles appears in the appendix to this book. The Rule is, as Gregory the Great first perceived, a very straightforward document. The appendix of this book offers the reader a number of modern commentaries on the Rule for further study.

1

The Rule of Benedict

> *Accordingly in every instance,*
> *all are to follow the teaching of*
> *the rule, and no one shall rashly*
> *deviate from it.*
>
> —*Benedict's Rule,* Chapter 3

The Rule Is Born

It was from world chaos that the greatest organizational constitution of western civilization—St. Benedict's Rule—emerged. The entropic decline of Rome and civilization in the fifth and sixth centuries caused the pendulum to swing toward order in other parts of society. St. Benedict (480–550) was a Roman who had seen the end of civil order bring moral decay. The lack of civil order had even affected the spiritual order of his faith and church. Benedict's first response was to run and isolate himself as a hermit. It may seem strange that a hermit would become an organizational genius.

But the role of hermit was a reaction, not a calling. Benedict had not lost his Roman love for order and organization; he simply wanted no part of a world lacking in it. A thousand years of Roman rule had left a legacy of order, and the Roman church had become the keeper of the flame of order. Furthermore, Rome had left a spirit of pride that the barbarians had not destroyed. That undefeated spirit would give rise to a new generation of revisionists such as St. Benedict and Pope Gregory the Great. The longing of these revisionists for Roman order ultimately would lead to the formation of the Holy Roman Empire and the Old Roman Order.

Benedict's calling was like that of the prophets of old— to return civilization to order, organization, and morality. Benedict prized the Roman skills of administration, management, and supervision. In particular, he saw these skills as fundamental to a good leader. In this respect Benedict saw leadership as being the result of order. Order, therefore, can result in great leaders. Finally, Benedict believed that administration, organization, and leadership could be reduced to Roman-style laws and rules. It is from this perspective that Benedict developed his famous Rule. The Rule gives a priority to administration and organization before spirituality; for this reason, it is timeless, cultureless, and favors no specific organizational discipline.

Benedict's Rule was first and foremost an international

organizational standard very similar to ISO 9000 today. The Rule supplied a set of operating procedures and instructions for organizational design, administration, job design, policy, and staffing—the efficiency of Benedictine organization went beyond spirituality. Benedictine organizations became the economic engines which controlled both Europe's manufacturing and its agriculture. Benedictine centers became information system centers and research centers as well, and the money they generated helped save western civilization. The Pope used their funds to pay off the barbarians and finance the rebuilding of the Roman Empire. To show how important Benedict's Rule was to the social fabric of the day, it is worth noting that the oldest copy of the Rule was "Codex 914," commissioned by Emperor Charlemagne around 800 to help design a new political order.

The Rule itself is believed to have been written in A.D. 540, near the end of St. Benedict's life. Benedict's Rule drew heavily on the earlier traditions of the so-called Desert Fathers, such as Pachomius, a fourth century former Roman soldier who developed a monastery and economic community in the Egyptian desert. While Pachomius' main motivation was spiritual, he learned that prayer and work were a natural combination, and his economic activities became as famous as his monastic order. Pachomius drew on his Roman military background, developing a decimal hierarchical system in which supervisors each managed ten people. These managers were known as

"Deans." In addition to his organizational structure, Pachomius built infrastructure via a written rule of policy and operating standards. There is no question that Pachomius deeply influenced Benedict's thoughts, particularly those on work and prayer.

Benedict's Rule was not above those rules inspired by the desert fathers. Benedict's Rule, however, flourished throughout Europe. The Rule initially spread due to Pope Gregory the Great, a former Benedictine monk in the sixth century. Gregory sent the first mission to England to spread the faith and, ultimately, the Rule.

The Rule's later proliferation was a direct result of Charlemagne's support and his application of it. Charlemagne envisioned it as a strategy to combine spirituality, work, community, and government into God's earthly organization. Many viewed it as part of Augustine's vision of a godly human city for all.

An Organizational Standard

Pope Gregory, a first generation Benedictine and biographer of Benedict, was the first to appreciate Benedict as an organizational genius. Gregory viewed the Rule as much more than a means to manage a monastery, and felt that any organization could find order through an application of this Rule. Gregory was an experienced administrator, having been the son of a Roman senator and a former governor of

Rome before embarking on his religious path. Like St. Benedict and St. Augustine, Gregory knew that order and stability were the prerequisites for missionary work. These three men had seen the collapse of civilization with the fall of Roman order and organization.

Gregory saw the Rule as a universal organizational standard with applications going beyond the monastery. He first used it to reorganize the Roman political and economic countryside. His economic organizations filled the granaries of Europe and the church. The Benedictine economic revolution in Europe is on a par with the later Industrial Revolution. This was a revolution that featured advances in organizational techniques, rather than the technological revolution that so characterized Industrial Revolution. Finally, Gregory reorganized the church's structure, and his Benedictine organization remains the structure of the church today. Using Benedictine principles, Gregory established a lean hierarchical structure of only five layers of management. Benedict's Rule promotes the efficiency of a lean hierarchy versus the inherent disorder of flat organizations. Today's businesses may find an old alternative to the downsizing mentality that has failed to save our industries.

The Rule's Application Today

Pope Gregory, and later Charlemagne, were the earliest to recognize the broad application of the Rule to organizations and administration. Today we see a longing for organizational order similar to that experienced in Benedict's time. In business, we see the international movement of ISO 9000, which stresses policy, procedure, and documentation. Business is coming to the same conclusion reached by Benedict—leadership is necessary but rarely sufficient to assure growth and longevity. These organizational keystones are found in policy, mission, procedures, rules, and culture. St. Benedict's Rule was clearly the ISO 9000 of the Middle Ages, providing a procedural model for the church, government, agriculture, and manufacturing. However, Benedict's Rule goes far beyond today's business standards.

Benedict's Rule is both an organizational constitution and a philosophy. In this respect, Benedict addresses organizational infrastructure as well as the heart and soul of organizations. If we continue the analogy of ISO 9000 as a procedural standard, we can put it in a modern perspective. ISO 9000 is only a small part of Total Quality Management (TQM), an overall philosophy stressing belief in quality. Benedict realized that laws and rules, while necessary and foundational, could not save Rome. That philosophy of quality and Benedict's view that faith must have priority over rules were the basis on which the Rule was conceived. We see this incorporated in the Rule where Benedict requires a searching of one's heart if the rule is broken.

The power of Benedict's Rule today is its ability to integrate rules and philosophy. This integration brings an understanding to rules and laws that allows obedience and loyalty. Obedience may seem like a strange virtue for western business, but there is a cultural foundation for it. The Rule was originally written in Latin and was based on scripture, and the original meaning of obedience was to listen intently and to respond. Obedience was a means of assuring the welfare of the community. It assumed moral leadership and even allowed voices of dissent at the daily chapter meeting. Like today's team consensus, obedience required the community to move on after an authoritative decision was made. Chapter 8 allowed for issues to be resolved by the community as a whole, but ultimately, its leaders bound the community. The magic of Benedict's Rule is its ability to convert the dreams of individuals and the community's mission into a common destiny. This is a concept I will discuss in more detail later in this book.

Benedict's concept of work and spirituality is also relevant to the modern world. The simple interdependence Benedict saw produced not only saints but also powerful manufacturing successes throughout Europe. Benedict took work and motivation to a new plane, supported by modern experts. A major group of management experts known as behaviorists see this as the ultimate motivation. The behaviorist Abe Maslow called it self-fulfillment or self-actualization. It does not require a "religious" connotation, although that was Benedict's leaning. Benedict's Rule can always be applied from a purely human approach.

The Rule is always pragmatic first because of its drive for order.

To summarize, an understanding of the Rule as simply *Ora et labora* (prayer and work) would be incomplete. More correctly, it should be *ora, labora, legel* (pray, work, read). The Rule promoted learning and information systems. Benedictine monasteries were true examples of what today we call learning organizations. These monasteries became knowledge-based organizations that excelled in innovation and invention. The Benedictine edge was in management information systems. Benedict managed technology better than most high tech companies to-

NATURAL DISORDER IN BUSINESS SYSTEMS AND ORGANIZATION

Scientists developing the second law of thermodynamics (entropy) in the twentieth century noticed a similarity to St. Augustine's fourth-century writings. These scientists had proven that physical systems naturally tend toward disorder. St. Augustine's writing on the decline of the Roman Empire in his book *City of God* showed that society and political organizations had the same tendency. Twentieth-century physical scientists, seeing this analogy, labeled entropy "St. Augustine's Devil." We know

day. We can learn a great deal by applying Benedict's model to our technology.

Managers will also find application in the design of international, corporate, and supply chain organizations. At its height, the Benedictine Rule detailed the operation of more than eight hundred monasteries throughout Europe and the British Isles. The Rule served to unify a single corporation which was itself composed of elements from a wide range of cultures. Information systems were designed to manage the Rule in the diverse organization. It was here in the tenth and eleventh centuries that the Rule helped bring about Benedict's vision of Roman order,

today that business organizations also tend toward disorder. Like physical systems, human organizations can affect this tendency, but it takes an input of "energy." Augustine suggested that this counter ordering required written rules, laws, and procedures for human organizations. Augustine, borrowing from the nearby desert fathers, developed his own rule for church orders. In business we see the same need today. Policy, procedures, culture, and leadership are entropy tools that can reverse disorder. It is in developing a "living" rule that order can be maintained—and this is the organizational genius of St. Benedict. ❖

demonstrating that Benedict's Rule is timeless in organizational design.

A Reader's Timeline

250–350	The Desert Fathers such as St. Anthony and Pachomius build manufacturing/spiritual communities.
306	Constantine emperor in East
410	Goths sack Rome
354–430	St. Augustine of Hippo
452	Attila invades Italy
455	Vandals sack Rome
476	Romulus Augustus—last Roman Empire in West
480–547	St. Benedict
529	Monte Casino opened
540–604	Pope Gregory the Great
771–814	Charlemagne, King of Frank
1964	Pope Paul VI names Benedict, Patron of Europe

2

Community as Organization

The workshop where we are to toil faithfully at all these tasks is the enclosure of the monastery and stability in the community.

Benedict's Rule, Chapter 4

When they are to be received, they come before the whole community in the oratory and promise stability, fidelity to the monastic life and obedience.

—Benedict's Rule, Chapter 58

The Concept of Community

For twenty-five years, the Japanese team organization approach to management has risen and ebbed in popularity. The attractiveness of team management is its promise to pull people together for a common goal. This is achieved many times at the expense of the individual, because the focus is unity and uniformity of purpose for the team. Japanese culture is highly suited for a system in which individual success is measured in terms of organizational success. Consensus is used to achieve unity within the team. These teams tend to be very "professional" in practice and application in Japan. The Japanese depend on this type of worker "professionalism" to select team projects that will have economic impact. American teams given the freedom of project choice tend to focus on working environment and conditions. The real problem of applying Japanese-style teams in the West, however, has always been the loss of individuality.

In my own career, I organized and nurtured a team at LTV Steel that won the first USA/Today National Quality Cup. For internal and external consumption, this was a Japanese consensus team. In reality, it was a true American team (actually a committee). The team was based on democracy—majority rule. In addition, it derived its mission and authority from my management position. While clearly modeled from traditional management-type committees, it was made up of both workers and management. The team's communal bonding was purely American, yet it outperformed hundreds of other LTV teams and American industry teams to win national prestige. This type of communal organization allowed for individuality while achieving organizational goals. It also filled the "social" needs of many employees.

Part of Benedict's genius was his integration of community, hierarchy, and organization. Benedict's communal organization achieved common community goals as well as individual goals. This balance is missing in today's corporations. In today's world, a "team" is a means of meeting corporate goals, not something to take care of individual needs. Benedict realized that for productivity, happiness, and in his case, spiritual self-actualization, individual and organizational goals must be merged. This moved Benedict to address such mundane things as sleeping arrangements, meals, and bathing in his Rule. His real genius was to deal with personal needs along organizational structure, leadership, and administration necessary for long-term success.

Guiding Principles of Communal Organizations

Benedict's Rule builds community before structure. Three principles are at the heart of Benedict's community: camaraderie, communal welfare, and stability. Benedict's approach to community is that it is the total system or universe. In this respect, everything and all of daily life are community. This approach is the same as that of Total Quality Management guru Edward Deming. In Deming's final and largest project—the U.S. Navy—his quest for quality required a major upgrade of personnel living quarters. This requirement was misunderstood by most, but Deming explained that quality is a total system approach and that includes the daily needs of the personnel performing the work. St. Benedict would have understood.

These Benedictine practices can affect productivity in a big way but their application is rarely understood. As I built community with that national award winning team, I had them meet every Friday for lunch. Lunch was a key part of the weekly meeting. The team had a $150 budget per week for twelve people. (The company president thought this was frivolous.) The team designed the menu on their own time and went to various Cleveland restaurants each week to bring food back to the plant. I had learned that this lunch was the major motivator for getting the crew out early on Friday. It also brought the employees together.

Benedict also brought employees together, an aspect addressed by his Rule. The Rule stipulates that the monks gather for a meal prior to working in the fields. The Rule puts a major emphasis on the community being together for meals. Chapter 51 of the Rule restricts members from eating outside the monastery without the approval of the abbot. Other chapters address tardiness to meals, travel, and the proper amount of food and drink to be served. A total of five of the seventy-three chapters address meals. Furthermore, Benedictine hospitality requires that all visitors be fed. It was over a meal that information was shared. Benedict was obsessed not with food but with the idea of people mutually sharing meals. It is an even older tradition that meals bind families and tribal organizations. It is a fundamental physiological fact that eating together helps people work together. Benedict further looked at other total system issues such as sleeping arrangements, work routines, etc., all with the purpose of building community.

The other guiding principle of the Rule is communal welfare. Benedict's approach was unique; it is not communism or socialism. Benedict's was a law of capitalism where profits were returned to the community. To that extent, it is a welfare system similar to our social security, Medicare, etc. At the heart of Benedict's Rule is a balance of corporate and individual needs. The outcome is the same ideal preached by those who advocate Japanese-style teams. The real difference is that Benedict used a total system approach. It is surprising to most business executives that Benedict's Rule requires strong discipline. Discipline and employee "re-engineering" are part of Benedict's view of communal welfare. Benedict's Rule does not tolerate grumbling; it requires obedience and loyalty with a smile. Benedict's communal functioning is not blind obedience or Japanese consensus but communal welfare. The abbot assigned a corporate mentor to unhappy employees. Employees (monks) who could not buy in were "excommunicated"—a mutual decision. The reason was that grumbling destroyed the heart of community and threatened communal welfare. This use of excommunication produced more unity than consensus ever could. St. Benedict's Rule was not as cold as it might seem. Excommunicated employees were always given two reproves and even welcomed back if they changed their minds. Benedict has one chapter concerning those requiring excommunication and one chapter on re-admission. We see that obedience/loyalty is fundamental to the Benedictine community.

Stability, in many ways, was the underlying civil theme of the Rule. Benedict had seen Rome after the fall and it left a mark on him. His Rule was to be a positive force to counter the natural tendency toward disorder. In fact, many of Benedict's writings are gone but his Rule survives. Benedict can be proud that his Rule, now 1,500 years old, is still used in organizations today. He clearly gave to orga-nizations what Rome gave to governments. Careful mem-ber selection and a rite of initiation requiring loyalty to the Rule first fostered this stability.

The Rule then became self-regulating for the commu-nity. All acts of disorder and disloyalty were dealt with sternly by the Rule. Benedictine stability goes beyond ex-communication. Routine is the methodology Benedict ap-plied. Routine gives security to individuals. They could count on daily meals, prayer sessions, and defined study and work periods. Even today, many experience the calm-ing effect of routine. In the military, young people come from a world of disorder and they are first given a routine at boot camp. Many of us find routine in our daily lives very comforting as well. Life routines do not lead to boredom but to security. Routine and schedule, furthermore, lead to organizational efficiency.

The Rule and Productivity

It may seem that the Rule's attention to physiological requirements such as dining and sleeping has little to do with business organizations. Benedict's genius, however, is in this total system approach to organization. In the 1950s, humanistic and industrial psychologist Abe Maslow confirmed Benedict's approach in his theory on hierarchy of needs. Practicing managers have always found usefulness in this hierarchy of needs. Maslow, like Benedict, believed that unless low level needs such as physiological and social needs were satisfied, workers could not be motivated to achieve organizational goals. Figure 1 shows the relationship of Maslow's triangle and Benedict's Rule. Communal organization is a logical approach to achieving productivity in many endeavors because it builds on common needs.

Furthermore, American manufacturing in the Industrial Revolution used a communal approach to various degrees. Steel, glass, auto, and mining companies supplied housing and food (The Company Store) for their workers. Charles Schwab, U.S. Steel's first president, even gave churches and community centers to the workers. These communal

Figure 1. Maslow's triangle and Benedict's Rule

practices played a key role in the high productivity of these early industries. Companies in our basic industries continued into the 1950s to address physiological, safety, and social needs.

I started my business career in 1971 at Weirton Steel. (At the time it had recently been taken over by National Steel.) Weirton Steel in Weirton, West Virginia, had always been a company community. Some families had worked there through several generations. Disability insurance was not needed; the company took care of its injured workers and unfortunate widows. The company made every effort to prevent layoffs, and management firings were like Benedict's mutual excommunication, only rarer. The company was loved by the community; its managers and owner were revered. Productivity and profitability were always increasing with the possible exception of the 1930s depression. But even then, the company and workers suffered as community.

In 1972 National Steel closed down this steel monastery at Weirton. The year 1972 was one of deep recession for the steel industry, and the beginning of a decade of general recession. Weirton Steel was then controlled by corporate giant, National Steel, headquartered in Detroit and close to the mills there. Weirton had seen worse times but this time it reacted as an economic organization rather than as a community. Layoffs and cutbacks were done in a cold and heartless manner. Managers were escorted immediately to the door by security personnel. Older employees were clearly discriminated against (opposite of a communal organization). The 1970s changed Weirton Steel forever. The worker/company relationship became merely an economic arrangement. Company and workers suffered, but no longer as a community. Loyalty, stability, and communal welfare were reduced to an economic exchange of work for money. In the long run, productivity suffered and has never fully returned. In worker/company economic arrangements, motivation is limited to that of the effect of more money. Work, therefore, is not a place for self-fulfillment or self-actualization. Unfortunately, this story is widespread in corporate American today. Yes, companies can operate as economic organizations, but they miss a real opportunity to maximize productivity when they do so.

Benedictine monasteries functioned during the economic tough times of the Dark Ages. They struggled and suffered together but more often, they became economic beacons. Part of this was because the Rule forced economic self-sufficiency as an organizational goal. Planning and investing for bad times were done in good times, not at the onset of the downturn. Steel unions, for example, after the great national strike of 1959, started a strike fund

AMERICAN COMMUNAL MANUFACTURING

The success of Benedict's communal approach was not lost outside the Catholic Church. From 1680 to 1880, a number of Utopian manufacturing communities arose such as the Shakers, Rappites, Zoarites, and Oneidans. Like the Benedictine manufacturing communities of Europe, these Protestant-American communities organized on similar principles. These communities successfully competed with capitalistic industry. Some products such as Shaker furniture

to cover just that problem. After twenty years, the U.S. steelworkers had enough to pay workers through a one-year strike. (The 1959 strike was nine months.) That was communal planning at its best. Benedictine monasteries planned in a similar way, storing money and food to sustain the community during difficult times. As we have seen, this built community by protecting individual needs. In good times, this maximized productivity.

Application of the Rule

I. DEVELOPING A COMMON DESTINY

The strength of organizational communities is their ability to pull all to a common destiny. That destiny involves the

and Oneida tableware exist even today. The Zoarites of Southern Ohio produced charcoal pig iron that rivaled that of the mills of Pittsburgh in the late 1800s. At Old Economy in western Pennsylvania, wine making excelled. Like the Benedictine monasteries, these communities found a balance in satisfying individual needs and community goals. They demonstrated the relationship between that balance and productivity. Inspirational writer T.D. Jakes said it best—"We work best when we feel the same pull of destiny. It is a magnetic force that pulls us together and unites us in common goals." ❖

individual and the organization. The Japanese, after the war, made the country a common destiny of the work-force. In a free economy, developing a common destiny means moving some of the focus beyond the organization. In the 1960s many U. S. plants found such mutual productivity increases by participating in the space program. Today, companies must look to products or customer services that can help with a common destiny. For a department, the drive is to move to a linkage with corporate goals and success. Tying corporate goals to the surrounding community is another way to develop common destiny. The key is to move beyond the organization into an environment common to the employee and company.

ST. GALL: FIRST BENEDICTINE CITY

The great plan for St. Gall was a new type of monastery that Charlemagne had envisioned. Charlemagne's city planner in the 800s was a Benedictine monk, Benedict of Aniane. St. Gall would be based on the Rule, but it would be a total economic community of both lay and religious personnel. It would be completely self-sufficient. St. Gall became the Pittsburgh of early Europe. It was a community with a complete steel making complex whose swords became famous throughout Europe. Its brass foundry

2. ADDRESS BASIC NEEDS

This again appears to be a difficult strategy for a company. For years, I have surveyed college students on what is important to them in a job. This has been done over the last ten years, which may have been the greatest economic boom in history. To my surprise, they consistently looked first for stability and security. Further research finds that the downsizing of the same period has had a great impact on them via family and friends. Companies need to come back to these foundation principles of St. Benedict's Rule. Organizations must build on Maslow's Triangle. Offering security will pay off in employee loyalty and productivity. Planning for bad times to maintain that foundation must be given prior-

also became famous for bell founding and for the massive bronze doors used in European cathedrals. An agrarian base, merchants, breweries, and bakeries supported St. Gall's Corps of Artisans. Monks were a small part of the population of the economic monster. St. Gall became the model for the European village as well as the European industrial cities of the twentieth century. These Carolingian economic centers were able to address all the needs of the individual (Maslow's Triangle) in a single community. Maybe more important was that St. Gall showed civil application of Benedict's Rule and its power to organize.   ❖

ity. Companies must follow the example of Benedict and the U. S. steelworkers of the 1960s and invest for future employee security. While there are many pros and cons, this nation's investment in social security has resulted in a basic trust of government (sometimes overlooked) which moved a nation out of economic depression. Companies need to invest for the long run and that includes employee security.

3. ELIMINATE NEGATIVITY

Benedict believed in life-long employment with one exception—grumbling. The Rule tolerates no negativity. Benedict saw the real Augustine Devil of disorder to be negativity. Elimination of negativity is for the communal welfare. What does the Rule call for in dealing with negative, grumbling people? Here Benedict's Rule is very specific. First, the rule calls for two reproves. These reproves are to be a sit-down with authority. A third reprove is called for if there is no improvement. The third reprove calls for a "punishment"—a pay cut, for example. Only after all this does Benedict call for excommunication. Clearly by this point, the "firing" is mutual. The Rule allows both the employee and management to come to a mutual understanding and agreement. Too many managers avoid a straightforward discussion of such problems. The first time an employee hears of the problem is when downsizing forces the manager's hand. Reproves are critical in addressing negative employees.

4. BUILD COMMUNITY

It has been in vogue for years to build and train teams. The Rule calls for an organization to build community. One simple Benedictine approach was communal meals. Today, we miss that opportunity to share meals. Many authors tell managers to wander around, but if you really want to know each other, eat lunch as an organization.

MODERN BENEDICTINE THINKING

The business community keeps on "downsizing," "rightsizing," "re-engineering," and otherwise firing people. I know guys who made the astounding discovery that the most successful companies in America treat their employees really well. Imagine.

—Molly Ivins, *Thank God It's Monday*

Value the organization more than the individual players.

—J. W. Marriott, Jr., *The Spirit to Serve*

The first order of business is to build a group of people who, under the influence of the institution, grow taller and become healthier, stronger, and more autonomous.

—Robert Greenleaf, *Servant Leadership*

Cafeterias should be clean and comfortable. Managers and workers should eat together to build community. Do luncheon meetings with the workers where the company buys. Meals relieve organizational tension. Christmas, retirement, and other company dinners add to bonding.

Another Benedictine approach was the daily "chapter" meeting. Management and the operating personnel should meet on a daily basis. This daily routine and employee involvement builds community. Building community requires managers to have access to learning individual needs. Then the manager can merge these into community goals.

3

Opus Dei: Work and the Human Spirit

"The Twelfth step of humility is that we always manifest humility in our bearing no less than in our hearts, so that it is evident at the Opus Dei, in oratory, the monastery or the garden, on a journey or in the field or anywhere else."

—*Benedict's Rule,* Chapter 7

Seeking workers in a multitude of people, God calls out and says again: "Is there anyone here who yearns for life and desires to see good days?" (Ps 34:13)

—*Benedict's Rule,* Prologue

A New Concept of Work

The monastic tradition going back to the Desert Fathers viewed work and spirituality as a two-way relationship. Work augmented spirituality and vice versa. Benedict actually put work on an equal plane with the prayer requirements. Benedict even went much further than a simple two-way relationship, proposing a symbiotic relationship between the two. Benedict saw prayer and work as needing each other in the monastery. Thus, his motto—*Ora et Labora* (to work is to pray)—became a standard of the Rule. It is in Benedict's view of this work/prayer relationship that we see a revolutionary approach.

The Romans viewed work as a necessity having no intrinsic value. Manual labor in particular was held in low esteem, resulting in the extensive use of slaves. Benedict required all, even administrators and craftsmen, do some manual labor, and this was a major break from Roman tradition. Benedict's ideas were more aligned with the Greek approach to the relationship between the physical and mental realms. Salem, a second-century Greek physician, said, "Employment is nature's physician and is essential to human happiness." In this respect, Benedict's Rule seems more Greek than Christian.

In Chapter 1 of the Rule, Benedict compares hermits and communities, the two major branches of monastic traditions. To Benedict, the superior approach is found in that of the Cenobites, which includes a work/prayer combination. His belief is closely aligned with St. James—"Work without faith is dead." Still at Benedict's time, St. Paul's writing formed the base for most practical applications of Christianity. St. Paul's writings saw work as a requirement of life and held it in high esteem. Paul, a tentmaker, used his trade to support his evangelical efforts. Even earlier, the Jewish faith put great importance on manual work, and Jewish rabbis were trained in a trade. Paul saw slavery (assuming moral and humane treatment) as part of a life requirement of work for some. We see Benedict's Rule as a major break with most Christian writers of the time.

While Benedict's Rule was a proven economic success for 1,500 years, his view of work had been lost until recently. One reason for this was the dominating opinion of St. Thomas Aquinas, who saw work as necessary evil. Thomas' organized thesis was directed at manual labor only. Thomas, a true workaholic, excluded white-collar labor. His view dominated western civilization until Martin Luther (an Augustine monk), who defined work as "God's calling." This became the concept of the Protestant work ethic in America. Today again, the Benedictine concept of work is back in vogue.

Work and Community—A Social Covenant

Benedict's Rule does assure a lifelong work covenant. Downsizing was not an option. The Rule and downsizing are not compatible. To Benedict, work is fundamental to our existence and community. Community is lost in downsizing because the common welfare is violated. A recent survey by Right Associates found that, after downsizing, only thirty-one percent of survivors trusted the organization. Worse yet, many researchers have found that survivors became less productive if they perceived the downsizing to be unfair. This observation is supported by many studies showing that the expected payoffs of downsizing (better stock performance, better organization, and reduced costs) are not realized. This is a Benedictine reaction because work is on the same plane of needs as are food and prayer.

The Rule requires an organization to supply and administer work. We have noted that work and spirituality have a symbiotic relationship and community was the means to foster that relationship. The Rule, therefore, is a social covenant of work with the community.

In the rare cases where this covenant needed to be broken, the Rule specifically calls for humane treatment. Since Benedict resorted to excommunication only in those rare cases where a mutual destiny and mission could not be achieved, the door remained open. Benedict's Rule also provided help on their new paths to those who were excommunicated. Today this means to use buyouts, outplacement services, and give clerical and professional help. Every effort will be needed to maintain trust and community. Former Secretary of Labor Robert Reich said it best—

"Trust is one of the most valuable yet brittle assets in any enterprise. So over the long term, it's far better for companies to downsize in a humane way." The Rule made a point of throwing you out in such a manner that you thought it was your idea.

The heart of the Benedictine approach, however, is how to avoid downsizing. This strategy of avoidance makes good business sense as well. Study after study has shown the benefits of downsizing to be marginal, and its impact on morale and productivity to be substantial. Benedict was well aware that community is a delicate balance of trust and shared destiny. The real energy and efforts of managers, therefore, must be to creatively avoid downsizing.

Humility and Work

In modern Japanese-style management, flat structure, uniforms, and equality of perks bring about humility. While the Japanese goal is Benedictine, its application is far from it. Benedict, like St. Augustine, had spent much time analyzing the reason for the fall of the Roman Empire. Remember, Roman law and order were cherished. Still, the layered privileged Roman social classes were self-serving and ultimately led to chaos. Romans separated themselves from work using slaves. Benedict cut to the heart to see the issue in Roman society as humility. His longest chapter in the Rule is on humility.

Benedict saw the Roman flaws that went unnoticed by most of Western Civilization for a thousand years. The Romans had a differentiated work system which required heavy supervision of untrained slave labor. To match their Greek mentors, the Romans veneered slave-built concrete structures to look like the precision stone cutting of the Greeks. This system of quick building by unskilled labor was a necessity to meet their massive empire building goals. This system distorted their political, administrative, and managerial systems, creating a system that strove for supervision rather than management. Good supervision achieved "ferset opus," a team effort among the slaves, but the supervisor was never to be a manager of associates. In the 1970s,

JAPANESE SPIRITUALITY AND PRODUCTIVITY

Kaoru Ishikawa is known internationally as the Japanese father of Quality Control. Dr. Ishikawa made much of the relationship of worker spirituality and productivity. Ishikawa attributed the phenomenal success of Japanese industries in the 1970s and 1980s to the tradition of Confucianism and Buddhism in Japan. In particular, he gets carried away (like Max Weber) in highlighting the Mencius strain of Confucianism, which he believed in. Writing on business, Mencius was a believer in a Benedictine-

the Japanese saw our use of unskilled employees as an extension of the Roman system in our Western culture.

Benedict's Rule preaches humility, employee involvement, democratic leadership, and hands-on management. Again as in all of Benedict's thoughts, humility was the cornerstone of community. Administrators and managers were to be what Pope Gregory the Great called himself—"servant of the servants of God." More importantly, managers were to love their job but not its trappings. Benedict required by the Rule that administrators be the best examples of humility in the monastery. Humility is a multi-dimensional virtue that is the holy grail of our modern quest for "team spirit."

Humility is more than the glue of "team spirit"; it is a

type system—"Whoever pursues a business in this world must have a system. A business that has attained success without a system does not exist." Mencius' concept that man is basically good allows for fewer supervision requirements. Ishikawa mistakenly noted in his books that Christianity's belief that man is evil accounts for the fact that fifteen percent of the workforce in the U. S. are inspectors, while only one percent is in Japan. Ishikawa's translator, David Lu of Bucknell, clearly and often voices his disagreement with Ishikawa's premises of Christianity. In reality, Ishikawa and Benedict are in total agreement on less supervision and more worker responsibility.   ❖

personal requirement of managers as well. No manager can excel at maximizing productivity without humility, because managers need to be advocates of the organization they lead or manage. Benedict realized that pride is the enemy of effective management. My own first job in management was that of assistant superintendent of a steel mill melt shop. I was a young first-time manager, managing seasoned steelworkers at pay scales as high as four times what I was making. I had several friends in similar management positions. The salary difference ate at their hearts, which, in turn, caused them to fail. In my own case, my goal, and I assumed God's will, was to manage—I would have taken another pay cut just to manage.

Pride can blind us and that impedes our ability to work with and lead people. One Saturday evening I was with these same friends in a mall in the steel town of Wierton, West Virginia. It was the 1970s and people were out on a Saturday evening. Most were in their Sunday best. One friend wondered where the steelworkers were. Seeing them daily in their old clothes and the natural dirt of the steel mill blinded him to seeing them cleaned up and in a social setting as steelworkers. Having come from steelworkers, I made no mental distinction. Mentally he saw himself as coming from a different class (a very Roman attitude) which allows pride to block dealing with those he managed in an effective way. This attitude prevented him from tapping into their experience and help, thus limiting him as a manager. Humility is at the heart of managing, while pride requires heavy supervision.

Benedict sees work, management, and job design as part of a communal relationship. To Benedict, work is too fundamental not to be fully shared. Benedict, therefore, required sharing of manual labor to some degree. The Rule, however, does recognize special individual talents such as those of artisans. The Rule, however, is tough on these highly skilled people if they fail to practice humility. Chapter 57 of the Rule states, "If one of them becomes puffed up by skillfulness in the craft, and feels that they are conferring something on the monastery, they are to be removed from practicing the craft and not allowed to resume it unless, after manifesting humility, they are so ordered by the prioress or abbot." Again, to Benedict, humility achieves the goal of team spirit without reducing the role of the individual. In today's team concept, individual achievement is ignored or "hidden" for the good of the team. Benedict allows individual achievement but puts the burden on the individual to blend it into community. Finally, administrators have responsibility to assure that this happens.

A Benedictine Model for Work

Ken Cloke and Joan Goldsmith in their book, *Thank God It's Monday*, reveal a well-known secret. "One of the hidden truths of our work lives is that we manufacture not

only cars and clothes, but ourselves through our work."
Work is as Benedict understood—an integral part of our
human nature and spirit. To the modern American, this relationship is costly. Problems, setbacks, and loss of work

THE PROTESTANT WORK ETHIC

The global success of the American Industrial Revolution left the world asking how and why. Max Weber, a German sociologist, supplies one answer in
what he called *The Protestant Work Ethic*. Of
course, men such as Carnegie and Rockefeller were
his role models. His logic relied heavily on Martin
Luther's view of work as "God's calling." There's
no doubt that Weber's model explained the American capitalists' and managers' never-ending approach to making money. However, it hardly
explains the productivity of the hard-working ethnic
masses. For a twelve-hour a day mill laborer to view
his lot in life as God's calling would be depressing at
best. Still, Weber's understanding of work and
human spirituality has much merit. Weber tended to
go to extremes and his final thesis concluded that
Calvinism was only spirituality for high productivity
and profitability. Weber and Benedict, however,
would today find agreement on the importance of
work (Luther's calling) to the human spirit.

take a huge mental and physical toll on us. Furthermore, managers miss the positive side of the relationship, thus losing the possibility of major productivity gains.

Benedict not only realized the relationship but also developed a means to tap its energy. Work is a social contract that evolves into community. Today we spend too much time trying to "legally" break that social contract. Once broken, the company suffers long-term damage to morale. Successful companies spend their time honing that social contract.

Once a company has created employment stability, true productivity gains can be achieved by climbing Maslow's ladder. Work itself can become self-actualization for us, given the proper environment. When this happens, productivity and creativity are unleaded, as we can see in the Benedictine monasteries of the Middle Ages. Of course, these gains come from the courage to face risk. It takes real courage to maintain stability in an economic downturn but that's the investment required in the Benedictine model.

Application of the Rule

1. AVOID DOWNSIZING

Having lived through twenty years of almost continuous downsizing, I know firsthand that it is a downward spiral. We try to hide downsizing in a variety of names, such as re-engineering, right-sizing, a second career opportunity, and others. We involve lawyers in downsizing to protect the company (a sure sign of a problem). We train on downsizing techniques and hire consultants. What is needed is the same approach to figuring out how to avoid it. One Benedictine approach is to involve employees in the problem. My experience is that employees will voluntarily take a pay cut to save jobs, and if they are part of the decision, morale actually improves. Furthermore, employees will search out waste if they understand that doing so can save jobs. Facing economic threats to the company as community is a powerful tool. It respects the social contract of work.

2. HUMILITY — NOT UNIFORMS

The problem with Japanese-style management is not in theory but that it is culturally incorrect. The Japanese administrate humility via uniforms, consensus, no offices, and no perks. Culturally, the Japanese style fits their country, where the common welfare is ingrained. A more efficient approach for Western culture is the requirement to train and develop humility in its mission. Humility can become a part of organizational culture and that's what Benedict's Rule did fifteen hundred years ago. Corporate culture can be used to assure conformance.

3. JOB ROTATION

Benedict's requirement for sharing manual labor is based on concepts of humility and self-sufficiency. It may seem to have limited application today but always with the Rule, it's not the form but the meaning. Caterpillar Tractor over the years required new college hires to rotate six months through all phases of the operation. Business consultant and author Tom Peters promoted the idea of marketing managers spending a week or two using their products in the field. I would go farther—an operating manager should plan on a week or two a year to actually work the jobs managed. It takes humility for a manager to show his weakness and lack of knowledge but he will gain understanding in the process and of the workers. Remember, a Benedictine manager is selected for management skills, not for knowing how to do specific tasks, a fact that too many managers and employees today fail to understand. Still the suggestion to work the jobs managed is not to learn how to do a specific job but to better understand the worker.

4

Leadership and the Rule

"Furthermore those who receive the name of prioress or abbot are to lead the community by a twofold teaching: they must point out to the monastic all that is good and holy more by example than by words, proposing God's commandments to a receptive community with words, but demonstrating God's instructions to the stubborn and dull by a living example."

—*Benedict's Rule*, Chapter 2

"The Rule's model of leadership and authority, then is a paradigm for any relationship— husband and wife, parent and child, supervisor and employee."

—Joan Chittister, *The Rule of Benedict*

Benedictine leadership is rooted in humility and administered by democratic processes. The Rule sets down specific qualities that a leader must exhibit. Benedict sees leaders as teachers and examples. The Rule requires leadership by example, not words. Pope Gregory the Great's concept of "the servant of servants" for leadership is a direct application of the Rule. In another view, a Benedictine leader is keeper of the worker/leader covenant and, therefore, a trusted administrator. The leader is also the chief arbitrator of the Rule. Benedict clearly loved the Roman military leadership model but adjusted it from his scriptural experience. What emerges is a new type of leader, one previously unknown to the sixth century. This new style leader changed the church and European government.

As stated earlier, Pope Gregory the Great was one of the first to apply the Rule to organizations. Using Benedict's Rule, Gregory defined requirements for church leaders such as bishops. Gregory's church manual, *Pastoral Care,* reinforced the ideal of leader as teacher. Bishops were not merely higher level administrators, they were teachers and role models. Benedict, like Gregory, saw St. Paul as the ideal leader. Paul's use of all types of communication to teach and to even administrate his ability via teaching was clear in his letters. Furthermore, it was the type of leadership missing in Rome during its decline.

Benedictine leadership is also flexible. The leader has the ability to interrupt and bend the Rule. Many authors have called the genius of the Rule its ability to change with circumstances. If a personal problem arises, leaders are called to listen first before applying discipline. As we have seen before, Benedict has a perfect balance of individual needs and communal welfare. It is the responsibility of leadership to maintain that balance. Benedict realized that people learn and grow at different rates. No rule, procedures, or laws could cover the differences and individual applications. The leader is empowered by the Rule to act as judge.

Authority and Obedience

We have seen that the Rule looks for the virtue of humility, but it also asks for the virtue of obedience from its leaders. Benedict's premise is that only those who have demonstrated obedience should be placed in a position to ask obedience. Again we see the influence of the roman legions in the monastic tradition. It's the idea that good soldiers follow orders. Failure to follow orders usually prohibits military officers from being promoted, and in the extreme, can result in court martial (the military's version of excommunication). In monasteries, corporations, and armies, obedience is needed to effectively implement strategy. Lower level officers must carry out company policy and strategy as part of their leadership responsibility. Chapter 65 of the Rule states, "The subprioress and prior (second in command) for their part are to carry out respectfully what the prioress or abbot assigns and do nothing contrary." Obedience and loyalty are requirements of a leader driven by humility.

Benedict is so focused on the relationship of obedience to the community that he dedicates a chapter to mutual obedience. First and foremost, orders of the prioress and abbot or of the subprioress or prior take precedence. After that, an "unofficial" obedience is required of senior members. Experience counts with the Rule. Senior members in today's business have lost that priority and importance. Benedictine organizations, however, tap that experience pool. In a lot of consulting with legal and research organizations, experience still counts and is reinforced by the title of "Senior Research Engineer" or the like.

Skills of a Leader

The Rule is specific about the virtues or qualities of a leader. The Rule also implies some skills necessary for a leader, particularly people skills and communication. It should be noted that Benedict required only humility and obedience, believing the skills would come with experience. While Benedictine abbots and equivalent leaders were elected for life, many an abbot had a shortened term due to poor people skills. In fact, Benedict himself was thrown out early in his career as an abbot. The Rule reflects this negative experience of asking too much of his average monks.

While most human resource people would tell you people skills are the top priority in promotions, promoted managers are often placed in non-people-friendly corporate environments. Swimming skills are of little value if you are placed on the football team. Again this is why Benedict sees organizational mission and culture as the driving forces for leaders to develop people skills. The Rule also helps to neutralize cultural differences that leaders sometimes need to adjust for. Benedict's Rule does not require skills so much as virtues. Still some people skills are needed to fully integrate leadership under the Rule.

A leader must be fully open to the idea of leading by participation. The Rule requires decisions to be taken daily to the chapter for discussion and consul. This type of participation leadership is not for everyone. In the 1980s, Sumitomo and LTV Steel formed an independent company (LSE). The new company was based on employee committees and participatory decision making. Managers were recruited from traditional operations, but less than a third of those managers (including Japanese) could function in a truly participatory environment. All of these managers had demonstrated people skills in a traditional environment. What was the real issue? Just what Benedict foresaw fifteen hundred years ago—humility! These unsuccessful managers grumbled about the "inmates running the institution" and tried to steer things from behind the scenes. Most current leadership models are based on a contingency theory that says that leader traits, behavior, and situation contingencies interact. The Benedictine approach reduces these interactions to humility and obedience.

Communication skills are another implied but not necessary skill of a leader. Today communication skills are desired because of their use in persuasion. The Benedictine model is both participatory and democratic, and thus, persuasion is not a high priority skill. Still, clear presentation of the issue to the chapter will be important for the chapter to arrive at a solution.

Communal Leadership

The Rule sets a framework for leadership. It looks at two factors in leadership—leaders and those who are lead. It demands humility of its leaders and obedience of the followers. In community, you cannot separate leadership and following because they have a common destiny or mission. The Rule puts the selection of employees on a level with that of the selection of leaders. Benedict reduced the qualities of both to humility and obedience. The only difference is that leaders are to excel in these virtues.

Benedictine Pope Gregory the Great went further, saying that "Obedience is the only virtue that implants the other virtues in the heart and preserves them after they have been so implanted." Benedictine Rule itself is both a testing and training in obedience. Being able to obey is a prerequisite to being able to lead. Earlier, St. Augustine's Rule also saw obedience as the "mother of all virtues." Benedict via his Rule (like Augustine and the Desert Fathers) felt that given the right community environment, these virtues would grow. This stands in contrast to today where we seek skills before virtue.

Many readers may feel at this point that Benedict's approach is for the religious and has little application in the hard, cruel world, but facts tell us otherwise. First, over the centuries monasteries have used society's worst to develop economic powerhouses. Second, Benedict's Rule has many similarities to our present-day military. Here the rules and regulations are taught and obedience required. Humility is taught in boot camp to build team spirit. Still the approach has roots back to the Roman Legions (like Benedict's Rule).

Stewardship

Probably Benedict's biggest break from Roman tradition was his concept of leadership. Humility and service defined the Benedictine leader. More recently, a similar approach for leadership has emerged, called stewardship. Peter Block defines stewardship as "a willingness to be accountable for some larger body than ourselves, an organization, a community. Stewardship springs from a set of beliefs about organizations that affirm our choice for service over the pursuit of self interest." This is pure Benedictine leadership, expressed better than even Benedict himself expressed it. The key to leadership is community. The real difficulty today is not so much whether stewardship is superior to leadership, but how to implement these two virtues.

Benedict developed leaders through a communal process. Training and commitment to the organizational Rule was the first step. The community was then responsible for selecting leaders with given guidelines such as the virtues of humility and obedience. The result was a true steward, or what Gregory the Great called a "servant of servants." Such a process is foreign to business. It is, of course, the ideal of

A BENEDICTINE GENERAL IN 200 B.C. (CHINA)

Sun-Tzu, Chinese general and author of *The Art of War,* was a pure Benedictine example. Sun-Tzu talks of obedience and common destiny as the establishment of leadership. Sun-Tzu's own words are "the ingrained execution of orders comes from being in accord with the legions." Furthermore, this great general talks of two ethical traits required for leadership—benevolence and justice. This might be considered the ethical equivalent of Benedict's spiritual virtues—humility and obedience. Sun-Tzu also addresses the importance of obedience, and sees "internalized obedience" as the trait of all soldiers. Like Augustine, Sun-Tzu sees obedience as the mother of all traits (virtues). Without obedience, military organizations break down.

democratic governments, but it is rarely achieved. Universities do have some of the Benedictine process in their professor-owned search committees for university presidents. Also, in some universities, directorships are elected by peers and rotated over a set number of years.

I must admit that I lack a simple and direct answer for American business. I must leave this as a challenge to the reader. Ideally, the Rule calls for peer election of leaders but I hesitate to suggest this. I would lose too many business readers who felt I had gone too far. The success of stewardship, however, requires the support of the community. Self-directed teams inside a traditional structure do not really represent a democratic process. The challenge of this century, I believe, will be to experiment with Benedic-

EMPEROR AND THE RULE

Charlemagne (742–814), a Benedictine capitalist, made the Rule a roadmap for a new economy. Charlemagne was a great admirer of and expert on Benedict's Rule. He envisioned a greater community of all of Christianity. His strategy—*renovatio imperii romani*—was the revival of the Christian Empire of Constantine (d. 337). Charlemagne embraced both the secular and religious factors of this greater community. In the Carolinian revival, monasteries became key economic manufacturing centers. The

tine leader selection. So far, we have talked about involving and empowering employees with one exception—the selection of leadership itself. The time will come that we will have to address this if we are serious about "empowerment." The Benedictine approach believes in full empowerment but it also realizes the need for leaders in the organizations. Benedict achieved this via a democracy, trusting in the Rule to assure harmony and direction.

Building a Culture for Leadership

Benedict saw leadership as a two-way process steered by the Rule. The Rule is the seed of a culture for leadership. Too much of today's approach is the search for a "leader"

artisans and smiths were not monks but were part of these great centers with living quarters and workshops. Blacksmiths achieved international fame in the forging of swords. The iron manufacturers of great monastic manufacturing centers such as Saint-Gall and Saint-Riquier became known as the "striking force" of Charlemagne's armies. Charlemagne showed the organizational power of the Rule as a management tool. The Carolinian economy would set the framework for the Industrial Revolution while Charlemagne's political application of the Rule built a foundation for the Holy Roman Empire. ❖

without addressing the environment of leadership. In turn, we demand too much of our leaders. We need to address developing an environment for leadership. Loyalty and obedience must be praised and *rewarded* as a corporate standard.

Since culture is the potting soil of leadership, it requires time and energy. New employees need an introductory training period (depending on size) for Culture 101. Companies like the Disney Corporation and IBM have been very successful with the approach. Benedictine novices spend the first year learning the Rule. It's worth the time for all involved. Many potential leaders fail because they lack a full understanding of corporate culture. The use of an assigned mentor is another technique to pass on culture.

Develop Your Own "Rule"

Some companies spend millions on employee benefit brochures and other training materials, but few even have an employee handbook of policies, expectations, and guides. I'm not talking about booklets on sexual harassment and such, but about cultural issues. What is expected to be promoted? Is there a written or unwritten dress code? What's the policy on missed days and late starts? What's the mission and corporate objectives? This does not need to be and should not be a legal document. In fact, the writing style should reflect the culture. The Rule should be part of the new employee training as well. Most of us spend years learning about corporate culture on our own. We have seen that culture is too important to an organization to be treated as an employee detective mystery.

MODERN BENEDICTINE THINKING

When patriarchy asks its own organization to be more entrepreneurial and empowered, it is asking people to break the rules that patriarchy itself created and enforces.

— Peter Block, "Stewardship"

Here lies one who knew how to get people around him who were cleverer than himself.

— Andrew Carnegie's Epitaph

More managers are reluctant to let their people run with the ball. But you'd be surprised how fast an informed and motivated guy can run.

— Lee Iacocca

Managers at all levels must return to their subordinates the authority they have slowly usurped over the years.

— Townsend and Gebhardt

Take a Step toward Benedictine Leadership

Assuming you're not ready to embrace a democratic process to select leaders, you still can move toward the ideal. A small step could be to informally consult senior employees about promotions to management positions. The university model offers another step toward the Benedictine way. For example, an employee committee could be used to interview and make recommendations on hiring new managers. Universities commonly use this technique because they have a better understanding of community. The recent selection of a president for the University of Toledo used campus interview sessions for all candidates. Hundreds of students, professors, and employees were involved in the process. Evaluation forms were used, but the ultimate decision was with the trustees. The University of Toledo went a step further, involving the greater community of the City of Toledo via the press in these sessions. That's empowering the community as well as using community. Benedict believed leadership was a product of community, not personal skills alone.

5

Benedictine Keys to Effective Organization

> *"Whenever any important busi-
> ness has to be done in the monas-
> tery, let the abbot call together
> the whole community and state
> the matter to be acted upon."*
> —*Rule of St. Benedict*

> *"All members of the community
> have a share in the welfare of
> the whole community and a
> responsibility for it."*
> —*Perfectae Coritatis*

One might agree that St. Benedict was a great organizer,
but can a modern manager use a system intended for
Middle Age monasteries? Clearly, Benedictine monasteries were the economic dynamos of their day. They were

centers of agriculture, manufacturing, and knowledge. The *Rule of St. Benedict* urged monks toward horizontal monopolies which provided everything from within and sold the excess. In many instances, these monasteries pioneered new technologies to expand these monopolies. Initially, these early monasteries were agrarian but rapidly pursued Benedict's quest for economic independence. Early successes of monastic economy occurred in fisheries, wool, milling, and horse breeding. These monasteries were knowledge-creating organizations where research and industrial experiments were promoted. By the 1400s, the monasteries of Europe controlled such industries as brewing, mining, grain milling, iron production, and glassmaking. In many cases the monasteries were industry innovators, as was the case with the earliest Cistercian monasteries of Britain, which pioneered deep coal mining techniques in 1140. In Saxony and Bohemia, monks advanced copper smelting and iron production. These industrial monks and their monopolies controlled Europe via industrial substations (granges), using lag labor where necessary. Great industrial corporations were developed including the Abbey of Foigny in France (1450), which operated fourteen water mills, three forges, two spinning mills, a brewery, and a glassworks. In many cases, the drive for economic independence led to great commercial inventors. Recent archeological finds of thirteenth-century English abbeys confirm the development of iron blast furnaces centuries before the Industrial Revolution. Louis Lekai, the leading historian of monastic industries, concluded that their success "was largely a by-product of the organization and spiritual aspirations of the Order." Their organizational effectiveness is their legacy to this century. At the base of this effectiveness we find a number of Benedictine organizational keys—harmony, teamwork, and stability.

Harmony

Harmony is never mentioned in the *Rule of St. Benedict*, yet it is the very essence of Benedictine community. It is the ultimate result of the Rule's obsession with obedience. The English translation of the word *obedience* implies "adherence in a severe manner." In the Latin root of Benedict's day, it meant, "to listen to." It is true that Benedict penalized for lack of obedience, but the rationalization was to maintain order and, ultimately, to foster harmony within the community. It is analogous to the history of military organization's use of obedience to build *espirit de corps*. Ultimately, habitual disobedience led to excommunication from the community, but this was not like some of the cold, escorted removals practiced by today's organizations; rather it was a mutual agreement with an open door to return.

While Saint Benedict's Rule is flexible on penalties for

disobedience, it is inflexible in the scope and intent of the meaning of disobedience. Murmuring and grumbling were the same as absolute refusal. Benedict reasoned that grumbling affected the community as much or more than a flat out "no." Benedict was not alone in seeing the problem of negativity. The Celtic rule (*The Penitential of St. Columbanus*) and the Rule of the early desert fathers also saw grumbling as a sin against the whole organization. Harmony cannot coexist with negativity. No organization can achieve its maximum efficiency if grumbling is widespread. Benedict did not suppress problems or personal freedom, but required that they be channeled properly through the organization via the daily "employee" chapter

THE CISTERCIAN CORPORATION

St. Benedict had originally set up his Rule to make each monastery an individual community. St. Bernard (1100–1153) was part of a twelfth-century movement that resulted in the ultimate establishment of 738 monasteries (and an equal count of women) for men's abbeys. Most were a newly-evolved order known as the Cistercian model, which built "colonies." These new monastic networks became economic corporations. To maintain organizational integrity, a General Chapter meeting of all abbeys was designed. This annual meeting lasted seven to

meeting, through mentors or the fatherly advice of the abbott (from the root *abba* meaning "father"). Benedict focuses in on what most managers avoid—addressing negativity at a personal level. What is lost to today's managers is the impact on productivity and profitability. Any manager who has tried to change knows the crippling power of negativity to bind organizations.

It has gotten so bad that organizations treat negativity and grumbling as a right and a personal freedom guaranteed by the Constitution. Recently, the University of Toledo was struggling through some difficult times. The new administration was constantly frustrated by the grumbling of professors who more often than not aired

ten days, consisting of abbots from all over Europe. Because of the huge size of the assembly, steering committees known as "diffinitors" were initiated. To build organization, a living mission statement known as the Carta Caritatios, the chapter of charity was read and hung at all abbeys in the order. The mission statement was supported by a code of regulations known as Initiates of the General Chapter. In addition to mission and standard operating procedures, a system of annual auditing by abbots was used to assure corporate integrity. This early corporate system is very close to the organizational principles of today's international standard—ISO 9000. ❖

their complaints in the local press. Such grumbling had seriously impacted the university organizationally as well as financially. The university president was publicly attacked for developing a list of negative professors. The chairman of the trustees made a decision to find the source of the negativity and eliminate it (a true Benedictine tactic). Ultimately, public cries of "educational freedom" cost the chairman his job. While his approach was politically incorrect, his effort was late but organizationally correct. Benedict used a process of discipline and a community spirit to avoid such an organizational breakdown and communal negativity. Of course, Benedict's biblical policy did not promote going directly to the sword but to pursue a policy of "reprove, entreat, and rebuke" (1 *Tim* 4:2). The real application of Benedict's Rule for managers is not to accept negativity as the norm but to aggressively seek to eliminate it. A manager must address negativity head on, and quickly. Like Benedict, managers must first be open to change and the possibility of a need to correct, but ultimately, if it is more a personality problem, it will require a stronger re-proof. It should be noted that when grumbling came from a widespread organizational problem, Benedict's open community daily counsel (employee involvement) corrected this. Failure to root out single negativity will first be reflected in a lack of organizational harmony, but ultimately, teamwork and stability will suffer.

Stability

Stability is at the heart of Benedictine community. Through mutual obedience, a family is created that is the infrastructure of Benedictine community. *Community*, as a word, has Latin roots meaning, "to eat bread together." The *Rule of St. Benedict* stresses the importance of coming together on a daily basis. This type of bonding was the foundation of community. Even business organizations require a measure of bonding to be successful. Long term successful organizations have strong social ties among their members. So many times business people overlook this key organizational facet. Socialization is bonding.

Stability is the organizational characteristic of strong bonding. Stability has long been a measure of business organization, and is generally expressed by the turnover rate. Business, however, viewed turnover more as an individual or department managerial measure than as a more global measure of organizational strength. Stability is, in fact, the last indicator of community strength. This is why Benedict promoted that the monk, even on a short journey, should return for the evening meal.

In the 1970s, I started my career as a metallurgical engineer at Weirton Steel in West Virginia. Weirton was the great steel monastery of its day. Employees worked their whole life at Weirton Steel. Generally, many generations of families had been employees. Employees were carried on the payroll in hard times. Communal lunches were encouraged. Family members got priority in hiring. Great community events were centered on Weirton Steel. Stock programs were very generous to promote employee ownership. Turnover rate was almost nonexistent. The recession of the 1970s and new corporate ownership broke that stable community with massive layoffs. Once the assurance of organizational stability was gone, the turnover rate increased for decades. There is a direct equation between individual obedience and loyalty with organizational stability. It is a bond and an organizational consent. Stability flows from mutual obedience and codependency. The early industrialists knew the relationship well.

Today, new organizations are trying to re-establish that convent of stability. Employees are "guaranteed" employment in difficult times. Social events are stressed as high priority. Stock ownership and gainsharing are emphasized. To some degree, this is a renaissance of the King Steel of the 1800s, when motivational communities were built in cities such as Pittsburgh by father-type industrialists. Stability also goes to the heart of management psychologists such as Abe Maslow, who saw job security as the basic foundation step to motivation in organizations.

Teamwork

Teamwork is another word not found in Saint Benedict's Rule. Yet teamwork is the end result of the Benedictine quest for humility. Teamwork today is an overused buzz-word for business. Teamwork personifies the true spirit of community where self is subservient to the good of the whole. Western managers, in their quest to achieve team-work, have imposed the culturally foreign concepts of Asian teams. The Asian team concept is one rule of the whole, not one rooted in sacrifice for the overall good. In the Asian concept, it is a duty to suppress self over the team. The Asian concept requires obedience but lacks the root of humility. The Benedictine model offers a democratic team approach based on individual humility and the necessary sacrifice. The Benedictine model does not require consensus of the group, only a belief in community by the group.

The Benedictine team allows for individuality but is focused on the community. The virtue of humility is much lost today. It does not suppress individual achievement but does suppress the use of achievement to control and use as power. Some of the greatest individual craftsmen arose from the Benedictine community. It is humility that gives the individual a perspective of self and a role to build community. Individual ideas are fostered, but ultimately the good of the community is the rule by individual choice.

The Benedictine team is much closer to the American sports team where individual statistics are noted and praised, but self-sacrifice for the good of the team is held in high esteem. Furthermore, self-sacrifice for the team ultimately results in a spirit that actually maximizes individual performance. It is this "spirit" that managers seek in teams. It is this spirit that is the hallmark of high performance organizations.

Benedictine teams are democratic in nature and function. A daily chapter meeting was used at the monastery to voice issues. Ultimately, the chapter was obedient to the abbot, but the abbot was bound by the Rule to take all into decisions. It is this mutual obedience that assured harmony and fostered teamwork. The Rule only created the environment for teamwork; it did not enact it by law. Benedictine teamwork is not a result of a structure—a committee format works as well as a "team." Benedictine teamwork does not require "training" but the creation of a communal spirit. It is the result of managerial actions rather than words. Many companies claim to value teamwork, but such claims are more likely to result in employee jokes rather than increased performance. Great teams, like great sports teams, are obvious. You can feel them in spirit. Their hallmark is a great individual having great humility.

Another characteristic of Benedictine teams is that they equate to community. The push today is to form multiple teams within an organization, which actually can lead to a breakdown in community and overall teamwork. Benedictine teams are totally integrated using committees for more specific problem solving, employee involvement, and administration. Benedictine communities used the daily "team" or chapter meeting to focus on one rule, one community. Committees were used to involve employees and develop a specific focus on an issue. Committees were part of the community, not separate teams as we see in many of today's structures.

Applications of the Rule

I. SET RULES AND ENFORCE THEM

Democracies are inherent organizations of laws. Our freedom and unity are established by laws and discipline. In business, an organization's harmony is dependent on mutual obedience and discipline. Rules should be clearly defined and enforced. Use an employee policy manual and train on it with new employees.

2. DEVELOP STABILITY VIA EMPLOYMENT

Stability is the cornerstone of a Benedictine organization. Stability is achieved through social ties and meeting physiological needs. The Japanese have lifelong employment, but American companies have achieved the same effect with a guaranteed year in economic hard times. Employees need that type of future stability to develop community or team spirit. Employment stability builds stronger organizations than variety in benefits.

3. IMPROVE ON STABILITY VIA FAMILY

Form strong social ties within the organization. Christmas parties and the like are important to build on. Remember the root of community is "breaking bread." Be generous in company dinners and lunches for retirements, company meetings, etc. where employees eat together. Use an employee social committee to involve people. Another important activity is a family day with picnics and ball games. Most important is to maintain these activities even in hard times. Cutting the budget first in these areas is a direct signal of instability.

4. ZERO TOLERANCE OF NEGATIVITY

Managers today are trained to address negativity being caused by the organization rather than the individual. Early monasteries learned that negativity has individual roots. Negative individuals should be "rebuked and reproved" early. Benedictine obedience for the good of community should be stressed in all training. If this fails, "excommunication" is needed for the good of the organization. Remember the *Rule of St. Benedict* called for kindness, guidance, and even support of the excommunicated.

5. USE EMPLOYEE COMMITTEES RATHER THAN TEAMS

Benedictine management allows only one team (the community). For specific focus or problem solving, the community chose subchapters as committees. Committees have fallen on hard times in today's "team managed companies." In fact, committees offer a way to involve employees while maintaining the overall team.

6. FORM COMMUNITY VIA OFF-SITE GATHERINGS

Community cannot be built on a nine-to-five schedule. A general "chapter" meeting of all employees every year is one approach to a better working community. A two-to three-day off-site general meeting to set goals, objectives, and renew mission is a great technique to build community.

6

Benedictine Art of Management

They (deans) will take care of their groups of ten, managing all affairs according to the commandments of God and the orders of their prioress or abbot. Anyone selected as a dean should be the kind of person with whom the prioress or abbot can confidently share the burdens of office. They are to be chosen for virtuous living and wise teaching, not for their rank.

—*Benedict's Rule*, Chapter 21

As cellarer (store manager) of the monastery, there should be chosen from the community someone wise, mature in conduct, temperate, not an excessive eater, not proud, excitable, offensive, dilatory, or wasteful, but God fearing and like a parent to the whole community.

> *But will do nothing without the order from*
> *the prioress or abbot.*
>
> *—Benedict's Rule,* Chapter 31

> *As often as anything important is to be done*
> *in the monastery, the prioress or abbot will*
> *call the whole community together and ex-*
> *plain what business is; and after hearing the*
> *advice of the members, let them ponder it and*
> *follow what they judge a wiser course.*
>
> *—Benedict's Rule,* Chapter 3

Supervision and Managing

Supervision is still a basic part of managing even though it is much maligned in today's touchy-feely approaches. The Rule clearly states its approach to supervision and managing: "The prioress or abbot should always observe the apostle's recommendation in which it is said 'use argument, appeal, reproof'" (*2 Tim* 4:2). Over and over again, the Rule uses teachers and parents as analogies for the manager. In the ideal of teacher and parent, we see the direction and guidance but also discipline when necessary. It is in reproof that managers are so lacking today.

Benedictine reproof, however, is a process, not a management style. Note that Benedict starts with argument and appeal but even more important is that all understand the full process to reproof laid out in the Rule. The process to excommunication requires two private reproofs followed by a public one. Actually Benedict devotes eight of seventy-three chapters to discipline. The punishments suggested are the only things that have little application today. Still we must remember that Benedict saw the manager as having a parental role. To rule out reproof would severely limit the ability of parents to mold. Like a parent, Benedict speaks of concern, love, and guidance in reproofs. Benedict realized that people climb the ladder to perfection at different rates with varying ability. He therefore left much of the discipline to the discretion of abbots and managers. The use of the Rule in training and the assignment of a mentor significantly reduced the need to use reproof. William Penn said it best about leaders: "They have a right to criticize but a heart to help."

Participation—Involvement versus Empowerment

The *St. Rule of Benedict* is based on the fundamental premise that whatever authority we have is for the common welfare. Leaders are but trusted servants. It may then seem strange that Benedict did not believe in what we today call employee empowerment. Empowerment would have been inconsistent with his hierarchical organization. In fact, it can be an entropic force in organizations, causing inaction and delay. Yet Benedict felt that employee input is at the core of the organization. His approach is what I call good old-fashioned management. I believe, like Benedict, that it is the responsibility of a manager to involve employees, to listen to them, and to take their counsel into his own decision-making process. Empowerment is but an alternative to poor management, and is not a substitute for good management.

The Rule has a twofold approach to employee involvement. First is to require and guide leaders to take employee counsel in decision making; second is to support a form for employee input. As discussed, Benedict looks for humility in leaders and managers to ensure that they are open to employee counsel. The Rule requires a leader also to counsel elders in decision making. The Rule calls for discipline of its managers who fail to show this type of humility. If these subprioresses or priors are found to have serious faults, or are led astray by conceit and grow proud, or show contempt for the holy rule, they are to be warned verbally as many as four times. If they do not amend, they are to be punished as required by the discipline of the Rule. Benedict, as always, uses the Rule to put the burden on managers and leaders. The Rule allows no default to empowerment for lack of good management.

The formal method that Benedict used for employee involvement was the morning chapter meeting. It was here that daily assignments and changes were made. Problems were discussed as well. The Rule requires teachers and managers to bring "anything important to the monastery." It requires open discussion but ultimately the decision is that of the leader. Benedict manages neither by democracy nor by consensus but by leadership. Both the community and leader are bound by a common destiny. Chapter is a mutual process that terminates in a decision by the leader to which all are bound to support by the Rule. The Rule again forms the participants and environment to assure it is a mutual process.

Let's look at the alternatives of this mutual process. Democracy as a process would prevent an environment of common destiny. Democracy would erode leadership in a nonpolitical environment. Employee democracy is impractical in managing an organization. Consensus would force an artificial destiny. Consensus ignores individual differences and, therefore, the need for strong leaders. It is only in the Benedictine process that community welfare evolves and still allows for strong leadership.

One of the more amazing approaches of Benedict's Rule is its tapping into the elders' experience without imposing overall discriminatory laws. This part of the Rule is unique in the use of the elders' experience in decision making. The Rule states the elders are to be consulted, but does not make such consultation the law. Again, Benedict depends on training and manager development to assure this is done in practice. Yet the Rule clearly states that "rank is never to be based on age alone." The Rule has here solved a problem we struggle with today. The Rule has a deep respect for experience, but does not build an organizational bias toward it. The Rule uses information but also implies legalism. In other words, a Benedictine manager is expected to involve elders as part of his role as manager. As we have been before, the responsibility is upon the shoulders of the managers and leaders.

Training and Commitment—The Heart of It All

The Rule itself is cybernetic, meaning that it steers the whole community as a system. It sets laws and guidelines and is its own disciplinary tool, and is, therefore, the very heart of Benedict's community. Besides its cybernetic nature, the Rule sets the infrastructure for a culture. As we have seen, both the Benedictine leadership and management styles depend on the culture, all of which makes the understanding and knowledge of the Rule as paramount.

The Benedictine approach is to first provide training on the "company" rule (policy and mission) until understanding is achieved. Then a commitment is required from the new member. The focus of the training is to come to a decision. Many employees today understand company policy but choose not to follow or implement it. Benedict requires closure on the training with a decision. This is close to the IBM approach—the employee must buy in to the dress code or leave.

The Vow of Corporate Stability

The closure on training in the Rule comes when the novice takes a vow of stability to follow and apply the Rule. This is a formal rite of initiation and it is part of building community. Businesses have shied away from such a formal rite. Still in most companies, the rite does exist but failure to take it results in a slow corporate death. LTV Steel had a very unique dress culture, one that consisted of wearing plainly-colored long-sleeve shirts. This was an informal but very clear dress code. I found it unusual since we were managing a hot steel making process. Employees who

CISTERCIAN MODEL FOR CORPORATIONS

St. Benedict never envisioned even the huge economic centers of Charlemagne in the 700s. The real growth, however, didn't come until St. Bernard's push of the eleventh century. Bernard moved these economic centers into corporate networks. Bernard's "corporations" became known as the Cistercian order. Benedict had originally designed each monastery to be independent and autonomous. Bernard developed a decentralized corporate structure allowing for the Rule to remain. A corporate constitution known as *Carta Caritatis* was added to handle

wore short sleeves were not part of the culture, and they knew they were making that statement. However, they did not fully realize that their careers were, in effect, over as a result of their failure to follow the code. That may seem extreme, but remember, they themselves had refused entry into the corporate culture. I now believe this was a rite of initiation—the company was asking for a vow of stability.

Before the novice was asked to take a vow of stability, a year of training was completed—training on the Rule as well as on the daily job routine. A mentor who was an elder in the community was assigned to the novice. It was the role of the mentor to see that all was coming together. The

the monastery corporate groups. A general chapter annual meeting was maintained to discuss corporate issues among individual abbots. This corporate structure assured the Rule was applied by allowing independent operations outside the Rule. The *Carta Caritatis* called for round robin visits and audits by the abbots. The model focuses on a corporate culture via the Rule while allowing some local adaptations. This model offers a unique balance of centralization and decentralization while maintaining a corporate culture. Culture must be centralized and enforced was the bottom line of the *Carta Caritatis*. After the Rule and culture, the left is decentralized to best fit the nature of the community.

mentor was another use of the experience of the community. Retention was not an issue in the first year. The primary focus of training was understanding, not indoctrination. Novices who couldn't buy in and left were a plus for the overall community. Today too few companies avail themselves of an initiation period. Retaining unhappy employees can be a real mistake for both parties. As we have seen, the Rule requires closure on training in the form of a commitment.

Flexibility—*Mobilis in Mobili*

Mobilis in Mobili is the Latin title Jules Verne used for his chapter on the submarine, the Nautilus (*Twenty Thousand Leagues under the Sea*). While the literal translation is *changing with change,* Verne was describing how this rigid submarine was built to accommodate changes in the ocean environment. *Mobilis in Mobili* is an outstanding description of Benedict's Rule. It supplies a rigid framework that allows managers to be flexible depending on the individual's progress and the conditions. It is not *laissez faire* or based only on the situation, but it is flexible. It is when I study such applications of the Rule that I am stunned by Benedict's genius.

Benedict solved a difficult organizational challenge—how can a "rigid" Rule take into account the individual and other factors. Benedict's answer was it was the role of a manager to properly apply the Rule. If we go back to the historical roots of the Rule, it is Benedict's answer for the decline of the Roman Empire, not their laws and constitutions but management. To have no rules is anarchy. To have rules without management is socialism, while having rules with management is the essence of democratic processes. Again we see the Rule as a total system approach to organization. Management is not viewed in isolation from the Rule itself. Benedict sees the Rule, leadership, management, and obedience as being interrelated, which takes us back to the importance of developing a vision, mission, and policy from which all else should flow.

Role of Middle Management

Benedict's Rule gives powerful support to the need for middle managers. Benedict assigns "Deans" to manage groups of ten. This use of deans goes back to the Desert Fathers and manufacturing units. In both cases, it goes back further to the Roman military that managed based on units of ten. Many today would be surprised that Benedictine organizations that were under a strong well-defined rule would need middle managers. Centrally-defined organizations might appear as great candidates for a flat infrastructure, but Benedict saw middle managers as organizational links.

Benedict's requirements for middle managers are loyalty, virtuous living, and wise teaching, but never rank.

Loyalty is the primary virtue desired. Benedict expected them to "share the burdens of" the abbot, not to simply delegate them. Organizational and personal loyalty are keys to the ability to "share the burden." Sharing allows no excuses such as "just carrying out orders." Sharing is the natural management style needed to achieve communal welfare. Benedictine middle managers share communal authority and, therefore, they must involve all in decision making. Benedict expects them to arrive at decisions based first on the Rule, second on the orders of the superior, and third on common wisdom.

Because middle managers are expected to represent common wisdom, the Rule addresses removal. Like all Benedictine management levels, middle managers are servants. The Rule is hard on those who manage based on this position. Humility rules, and breaks in humility are not tolerated by the Rule.

Applications of the Rule

1. CREATE A WELL-DEVELOPED NEW EMPLOYEE TRAINING

Probably one major corporate oversight is a well-developed new-employee training program. When business conditions are such that there is a need to fill jobs, employees are put quickly into the fire to keep things running. This causes the overall community to suffer. We have seen that Benedict's organizational success is based on the understanding and acceptance of policy and procedures. A new employee needs a written "Rule" and initial training on it. This initial training must have priority and be prepared. The Benedictine view is that system itself is dependent on the quality of this training. Training is, therefore, central to the role of management.

2. ASSIGN SENIOR MENTORS

We have seen that the Rule requires the use of mentors and informal involvement of elders. Many companies have the opportunity to blend these objectives. Doing so provides a critical role for senior employees that is not part of management. Benedict believed that organizational experience was a major asset to be utilized. Mentors offer a channel to use this asset. The mentor program should be designed formally and managed. In too many companies the mentor program is informal and, in reality, nonexistent.

3. DEVELOP A RITE OF INITIATION

Benedictine philosophy views the initial training and mentoring as a process that leads to a commitment. That process is monitored and corrections made. The first year is a time of mutual probing. This period should be carefully managed. Concerns for both parties need to be addressed quickly. Too many early misunderstandings threaten communal welfare. The mentor should be active on a daily basis to lead the new employee. Finally, at the end of the first year, both parties should make a commitment. Benedictine stability demands that at least an informal commitment be made.

4. CONSIDER ROTATION FOR FRONT LINE SUPERVISION

Geese are an excellent example of leadership rotation in nature. Flying in formation, the leader carries the burden for the flock that flies with ease due to the V formation. Ultimately, the leader will tire and be replaced. Rotation is possible at lower levels of management. Department chairs are routinely elected and rotated every three years. Foremen and crew leaders are sometimes successfully rotated as well. If someone would excel, then he or she could be moved into a permanent management position. For some supervisory positions, rotation offers assurance of communal welfare as well as a potential testing ground. Rotation assures humility and self-sacrifice. Of course at the higher level, rotation becomes counter productive to stability.

7

The Benedictine
Learning Organization

> *Idleness is the enemy of the soul. Therefore, the community members should have specified periods for manual labor as well as for prayerful reading.*
>
> —*Benedict's Rule,* Chapter 48

> *On Sunday all are to be engaged in reading except those who have been assigned various duties.*
>
> —*Benedict's Rule,* Chapter 48

Lectio Divina

The Benedictine motto of work and prayer is somewhat misleading if you assume a 50-50 split. Benedictine monks did not go around chanting for half the day. Benedictine prayer does include chanting, but much more time is dedicated to *Lectio divina* (spiritual studying). Benedict's Rule searches for excellence in prayer, work, and learning. *Lectio divina* was the Benedictine path to improved prayer. Reading and meditating on the scripture deepened prayer more than daily repitition could. *Lectio divina* brought a new type of excellence to prayer. In this basic principle, Benedict built a foundation for the learning organization.

A learning organization must be based on mission and supporting organizational procedures for learning. The Rule did precisely this. "Learning organizations" are in vogue today, but generally they lack organizational infrastructure. The Rule required a minimum of two hours of study per day. Try to imagine any organization today giving even one hour a day to employee creative free time. Benedict proved that such a policy paid back many times. Benedict's spiritual success paved the application of the learning organization in all types of human endeavors. Benedictine successes included art, architecture, literature, metal smithing, agriculture, and manufacturing. All of these great accomplishments started with a few monks with a love of learning. The story fits well what Margaret Mead once said: "A small group of thoughtful, committed people can change the world. Indeed, it is the only thing that ever has."

Information Systems

The Rule with its inherent balance of work, prayer, and study provided the foundation for the pursuit of learning. Even so, early Benedictine monasteries lacked a network or system to create knowledge. That network came in the first half of the twelfth century with the dynamic reformer St. Bernard. His reformed Benedictine order, known as the Cistercian Order, had more than 350 monasteries, located in every European country, by 1250. Bernard promoted a corporate approach where parent monasteries started new "daughter" monasteries. Bernard also applied the Rule on a corporate basis with an annual general chapter meeting. At first, this new corporate network assured that Benedict's Rule was applied uniformly. Soon the new corporate charter (*carto caritates*) called for exchanging visits and corporate management.

The new network led to a new potential on the order of today's Internet. Monasteries could exchange and copy manuscripts. The Rule's basic promotion of study led to a demand for more books. Remember, this was before the printing press in a time of hand copying. It is estimated that it could take up to a year to make a single copy of the Bible.

Another part of Benedict's philosophy that gave information roots was the drive to be self-sufficient. It was this principle of self-sufficiency that propelled Benedictine monasteries into all phases of agriculture and manufacturing. For example, expertise in wool manufacture led first to grain production, then animal husbandry. This was followed by the manufacture of shears to cut the wool, which ultimately led to the manufacture of iron. Finally, this inspired the development of our mining. Moving into these new areas of endeavor required information, and improving productivity required the creation of knowledge. The great Cistercian movement resulted in the development of monastery book lists, and finally, a Cistercian database. While civilization slept, the Cistercian database advanced knowledge. As this database increased, the lending and sharing of books became a limiting factor.

The need to copy books and manuscripts as well as the need to document new knowledge spawned an information center—the scriptorium. These monastic copying centers allowed information to be disseminated as well as a body of knowledge to be created. This information network allowed major advances in technology throughout the monasteries of Europe. We must not forget that the root of this information explosion wass the Rule and its requirement for study and improvement.

The scriptoriums and book lists formed the information network needed to create knowledge. In 1195, a new database was developed—the *Hortus Deliriarum*—which was an encyclopedia. The Benedictine principle of information dispersion that leads to knowledge creation was integral to technological advances. The next step in this process was the publishing of new knowledge. In the metal smithing and arts, a type of textbook was developed—*Schedula Diversarum Artium*. By the end of the 1200s, ore mining was being advanced rapidly based on Cistercian textbooks and experimentation. Many of these mining techniques are still in use today.

Visual Learning

Benedictines were a learning community. Their leaders were teachers, their libraries were databases, and the Rule fostered study. In addition to their development of databases, libraries, divine study, and scientific study, the Benedictines used visual learning and illustration. Benedict had borrowed the use of color from its use in Roman law. Written laws were written in a red orche color and called *Rubries* (from the Latin *rubrica* for red). Illustration and color became an important part of the scriptorium crafts. Most people are visual learners, and the Benedictines invested heavily in the use of visual techniques. Illustration as a learning tool spread through Europe in church windows and in art.

A Learning Organization

Peter Senge is his book on the learning organization (*The Fifth Discipline*) said there are five disciplines of a learning organization. Senge's five disciplines can be compared directly to Benedictine concepts below.

Learning Discipline	Benedictine Principles
Systems Thinking	The Rule
Personal Mastery	Excellence in Work
Mental Models	Lectio Divina
Shared Vision	Community
Team Learning	The Leader as a Teacher

Most of today's experts on learning organizations would agree with Benedict that it all starts with individual learning. Individual learning is followed by the building of a culture and environment for learning. Benedict saw the abbot as being responsible for the development of that environment. When Benedict looked at the leader as a teacher, it was not the role of teaching but that of learning and education he envisioned. The Benedictine leader takes shared destiny and builds a vision for learning. John Kennedy did this when he made it a national goal to reach the moon. Kennedy's vision would translate into a giant leap in learning. It jelled a national system that brought science and engineering to the forefront in learning and created a desire to learn. Benedict did that same thing, creating a knowledge engine for Europe and Western civilization.

The Benedictine learning organizations started with individual creativity assured by a daily study time. Canadian Railways is a modern example of the Benedictine learning organizations. In the early 1980s, the company made the decision to buy personal computers for most of its employees. This was at a time when computers couldn't even effectively compete with good electronic typewriters. Employees were given time to experiment and find applications. The end result was a completely computerized system within five years and a knowledge database filled with employee skills. Compare this to LTV Steel in the early 1990s; purchase of computers was restricted because people might "waste time playing games," according to a company vice-president. LTV clearly had a leadership problem and is a good example of how organizations destroy learning. Organizational learning requires giving freedom to employees to be creative. This was the Benedictine advantage—individual time for creativity.

Knowledge Creation

Learning organizations create knowledge. Benedict's Rule had set the infrastructure for learning. St. Bernard supplied an information highway via scriptoriums in the 1100s. By the 1200s, this corporate learning network was amassing knowledge at a rate never before seen. Monasteries gained competitive advantage in wool making, wine making, mining, metalwork, fishing, agriculture, ore smithing, and most manufacturing. This exponential growth of knowledge required one other Benedictine concept of shared learning and skills: The Rule favored dispersion of knowledge rather than compartmentalized expertise.

In many areas of Europe the monasteries' major competition came from craft guilds. Craft guilds were learning organizations, but they hoarded knowledge instead of sharing among similar groups. They also limited information distribution by passing down procedures orally instead of through the printed word. Craft guilds did produce excellence in techniques and artistic expression, but they gave few technological breakthroughs to society. The Benedictine monasteries were knowledge-creating centers, sharing and distributing knowledge as well as doing research and development.

Many companies today use the craft guild model. They work in secrecy and block information exchanges on most levels, using technological advances for short-term gain instead of long-term cooperative advantage. Republic Steel in the 1970s had a number of divisions that had pioneered new steel products. One superior product for machining invented at the Chicago facility was patented and became the heart of Republic's corporate success. The Chicago plant for years would not share that technology with their Canton plant. In the 1980s the Chicago plant closed and the product was transferred to Canton. The Canton plant struggled to produce the steel, because even then Chicago management was holding back. Meanwhile, the field quality of the product dropped dramatically, accelerating the company to bankruptcy. That is an extreme example of poor knowledge creation.

Applications of the Rule

1. PAY FOR SKILLS

There is a movement in the United States of new work systems designed to pay for skills. At a joint venture in Cleveland (LSE), I took part in an experimental agreement between the company and union (United States Steelworkers) to pay for skills as opposed to seniority. Employees progressed in job level and pay according to their training and skill attainment. It was a great experience to see this approach transform the company into a learning organization. Pay for skills not only increased productivity, it greatly enhanced creativity. Technology changes came rapidly from this highly skilled operating core. Operators developed, wrote, upgraded, and maintained operating procedures based on this learning and increased knowledge. Employees also were given time to develop corporate guidelines. If you want a learning organization, your pay system needs to reflect that goal and mission. A byproduct of this was that employees became multi-skilled in crafts. The skills of the electrician, millwright, welder, and others were combined through training into super-craft positions that actually reduced manpower requirements. The super-craft position offered high pay and at the same time reduced overall corporate costs. Furthermore, the company pursued the Benedictine principle of self-sufficiency, and line operators were trained in basic maintenance work. The results of pay for skills were fewer people, higher pay for those people who were there, greater self-sufficiency for the workforce, enhanced learning, and superior knowledge creation.

2. GAINSHARING

Gainsharing is pure Benedictine for a number of reasons. First, it assures a communal approach to rewards. Second, it focuses on learning and knowledge creation. Gainsharing differs from profit sharing in that the area of gain—selected jointly by employees and management—can be factors such as quality, environment, safety, and the like.

FIRST STEEL MILL, NORTH YORKSHIRE, 1538

"If Henry VIII hadn't expelled the monks, the Industrial Revolution might have started at the abbey in North Yorkshire." This was the conclusion of a recent British archeology team. One of the abbeys closed by Henry VIII—Rievaulx Abbey at North Yorkshire—was operating a prototype of a blast furnace built two hundred years before blast furnaces ushered in the Industrial Revolution. The structures

Gainsharing is generally communal in design as well as payment. At LSE, company quality goals, for example, led to an eighty percent decrease in customer complaints. Gainsharing is one of the best communal techniques available today. Gainsharing allows the community to focus on tactical goals that ultimately contribute to profitability. It allows the organization to learn and create knowledge. Coupled with pay for skills, it can transform an organization into a learning center.

3. KNOWLEDGE SHARING

The exponential growth of knowledge in the monasteries during the 1200s was a direct result of knowledge sharing. Books were borrowed and copied. The General Charter called for visits between monasteries to exchange ideas.

suggest a very powerful furnace with a water driven bellow system. The team archometallurgist reported, "We know that the Cistercians were innovators, and technologically they were very astute." Resources in the area continued with a forging complex four miles from the abbey at Rievaulx, which may have been used to forge iron and steel. North Yorkshire's core business was wool production, and the abbey maintained over 14,000 sheep. Driven by self-sufficiency, the abbey became a producer of sheep shears and, ultimately, fine steel.   ❖

Today, companies such as Syn-Optics use similar techniques, promoting division luncheons every quarter to exchange ideas between corporate areas. Sharing over meals

MODERN BENEDICTINE THINKING

Organizations learn only through individuals who learn.

—Peter Senge, *The Fifth Discipline*

The desire to create is not limited by beliefs, nationality, creed, educational background, or era. The urge resides in all of us . . . it is not limited to the arts, but can encompass all of life, from the mundane to the profane.

—Robert Fritz, *Path of Least Resistance*

Innovation and creativity are the lifeblood of a firm's existence and the source of future profits. They germinate only in the fertile soil of the human mind.

—Ernest and Young, *Executive Manual*

The skills of the work force are going to be the key competitive weapon in the 21st century.

—Lester Thurow, *Head to Head: Coming Economic Battle*

is always Benedictine. Major corporate research centers in the basic industries have information Fridays with informational talks on technology available for all in the corporation (a schedule is sent out quarterly). Universities commonly have research sharing forums on a weekly basis to update all. Newsletters, forums, and lunches are but a few ideas; the key is to share information throughout the company. Industry conferences are also important, but that information must be networked, meaning that employees attending conferences should report back to all on the information and knowledge gained. Sharing information leads to knowledge creation.

8

Benedictine Quality

When they live by the labor of their hands, as our ancestors and the apostles did, then they are monastics.

—*Benedict's Rule,* Chapter 48

If monastics commit a fault while at any work—while working in the kitchen, in the storeroom, in serving, in the bakery, in the garden, in any craft or anywhere else—either by breaking or losing something or failing in any other way in any other place, they must at once come before the prioress or abbot and community and of their own accord admit their fault and make satisfaction.

—*Benedict's Rule,* Chapter 48

All humility should be shown in addressing a guest or animal or departure. By a

> *bow of the head or complete prostration of*
> *the body, Christ is adored and welcomed*
> *in them.*
>
> *—Benedict's Rule,* Chapter 53

Community as a Basis for Quality

A sense of community is a powerful motivator for quality. We see this even today in Shaker furniture and Mennonite carpentry. Community values pride in work over the individual. This is the type of effort that cannot be talked into existence via teams, because it runs deeper. This is pride in being a member of the community and in claiming ownership of the product and service. This is the type of pride that makes employees want to tell the world where they work.

The Benedictine motivation for this type of community quality was noted in ownership and reinforced by the discipline of the Rule. The problem most of us face today is the development of that sense of ownership that Benedictine operations had. St. Benedict realized that communal ownership meant communal quality. This, of course, is the ultimate goal of today's team approaches. As we have seen before, Benedict captured the "team" goal using methodology different from that of today. Community goes beyond teams in that ownership is shared.

Ownership is a constraint, of course, today. Even profit

sharing does not always build a sense of ownership because the ownership is too remote. "Employee-owned" companies have also failed to develop the Benedictine sense of true community ownership. The closest approach we have today to Benedictine ownership in quality is gainsharing. Gainsharing is not corporate ownership, but it is ownership of capital gains. My own experience has shown dynamic correlations between the use of gainsharing and the attainment of quality. Allowing employees to share in the improved profit of quality can be a powerful motivation. At LSE Company in Cleveland, returns due to poor quality accounted for 20 percent of the product price. The use of gainsharing objectives cut that cost to less than 1 percent. To the employee, that resulted in an additional $15,000 to $20,000 a year in gainsharing checks.

The key to Benedictine quality is to make individual effort part of the community. Benedictine monks produced beautiful artistic copies of books. Each book might take a full year of effort. There was no individual recognition for this painstaking effort, but there was recognition of the quality of the community.

Benedictine quality could be seen not only in products, but also in service. Hospitality to all was a requirement of the Rule. Visitors to any monastery could expect food and lodging. The virtue and principles of hospitality are based on Christian principles; however, there were side benefits. Travelers exchanged ideas, brought news, and could carry information. Hospitality gave support to the Benedictine information highway.

Honesty—The Touchmark of Process Quality

At the heart of Benedictine process quality is the idea of doing a job right the first time, but Benedict realized that this was only an ideal. People will make mistakes, and these mistakes are the root of quality problems. My own experience of being a quality control manager taught me that simple mistakes caused almost all quality problems. Even worse, one or more employees almost always know about these mistakes. A lack of honesty and a sense of fear cause such mistakes to go unreported until final inspection, or sometimes even after delivery to the customer. Quality guru Edward Deming well understood that fear of reporting problems was a significant factor in poor quality. The Rule focused not on getting people to get it right the first time or even every time, but on getting people to report their errors and mistakes. The Rule then required a more forgiving approach from managers. Discipline was more strict for not reporting errors than it was for making them.

Quality is part of the community concept. Quality is, therefore, the responsibility of everyone. Self-inspection is the first defense but ultimately everyone involved in a process must be an inspector. Management performed inspection as well. Discipline was implemented according to the

Rule in cases of poor quality. Today we avoid discipline but community requires it to function properly. Making an honest mistake was not the real issue; the issue was covering up that mistake. The recent quality problems of Firestone can be traced to the fear of reporting mistakes that is felt by a number of employees.

Inspection and Process Control

Benedictine concepts of quality agreed with most quality gurus that quality requires an attitude as well as written procedures. The Rule, however, still called for inspection and discipline because it accepted human nature as nonperfect. Too many companies today believe that Total Quality Management makes inspection an obsolete function. Benedict believed that process control, even with documented procedures, would tend toward disorder. His Roman background helped him understand well the natural entropy human element. Benedictine inspection is cybernetic and diagnostic. It focuses not on sorting out bad products but on making system and human adjustments to the process to eliminate factors which create poor quality.

Through this cybernetic approach, Benedictine monasteries achieved excellence in art, architecture, manufacturing, and crafts. The only secrets required were concepts of community, self-inspection, elimination of fear, and ultimately, discipline as noted by inspection. Most importantly,

Benedict saw human excellence as a system problem, not as an individual problem. Benedict saw community, the Rule, and discipline as the guide to taking the system to excellence.

This does not mean that he overlooked the individual. Discipline was focused on the individual but only because these were instances where the individual did not conform to community. Mentors were the keys to bringing excellence to art and manufacturing.

Applications of the Rule

I. DIAGNOSTIC INSPECTION

Quality expert (and my former boss) Roger Slater stated in his book that the number one myth in quality is "You can't inspect quality in." Like me, he had done exactly that. Inspection does work; the real issue is at what cost. Benedictine thought is pure process control but it does not eliminate inspection. Inspection is part of the process of excellence. Excellence demands review as a basis for improvement. Benedictine approaches clearly reject the sort inspection method, but do incorporate the idea of diagnostic inspection. Diagnostic inspection focuses on process correction and defect prevention. Furthermore, discipline is part of the "process" correction. Excellence requires this combination of diagnostic inspection, disciplinary correction, and community responsibility in products and services.

2. COMMUNITY INSPECTION

One very powerful part of Benedictine concepts of quality is that quality is the responsibility of everyone. Job rotation in the monastery forced monks to be workers, inspectors, and managers. At LSE Company in Cleveland, I had the opportunity to design a job rotation program that forced operators to be inspectors and vice versa. This was a practical application of Benedict's Rule. Inspector/operator employees can approach diagnostic inspection intelligently because they know the process. Inspectors who do nothing but inspect become very good at sorting out bad products (and services), but lack the knowledge needed to find the root cause in the process. Traditional quality control managers fear this approach at first, but as I did, learn to see its true advantages. The same is true for making managers periodically do some of the work for "educational" reasons.

EXTREME DISCIPLINE IN THE CRAFTS

Middle Ages stone masons were serious about quality and affected by Benedict's Rule. In the building of cathedrals, the biggest mistake a mason could make was to ruin a stone. The masons were paid after inspection by the paymaster. They were given a bonus for good quality and pay was subtracted for

3. DRIVE OUT FEAR

This is one of quality guru Edward Deming's famous fourteen points. The Benedictine focus was always on self-inspection. Reporting poor quality, mistakes, and errors is the responsibility—actually duty—of all. Employees must feel free to report their mistakes. Mistakes and errors are often the root causes of poor quality. Reporting them early can help avert major disasters such as the Firestone Tire crisis.

4. DISCIPLINE WHEN NECESSARY

Discipline may seem inconsistent with driving out fear, but remember that the concept of community makes this traditional view obsolete. Mistakes and errors should be treated with humility, but lack of concern for the Rule or community requires discipline. You can expect employee errors

poor quality. In cases where the problem appeared to be more than a simple error, more extreme punishments were applied. The ruined stone was placed on a bier and covered with black cloth. The guilty mason was dressed in the cloak of a mourner and made to "pray" at the stone's burial. Brother masons might even apply physical beatings. In any case, the mason was forced to quarry and shape a new stone before being accepted back into the brotherhood. Once a stone was fully replaced, all was forgotten. ❖

and all can learn from them, but poor attitude cannot be tolerated. Discipline is the responsibility of management. Furthermore, the scope of discipline must be left, as it is in Benedict's Rule, to the discretion of the manager. Termination limits (excommunication) can be designed in the corporate Rule. Attitude issues can be difficult to change, and termination must be the final option when all else fails.

9

The Larger Community

*All members of the community have a
share in the welfare of the whole community and responsibility for it.*

—Perfecta Caritatis

*Great care and concern are to be
shown in receiving poor people and
pilgrims because in them more
particularly Christ is received; our
very awe of the rich guarantees them
special respect.*

—Benedict's Rule, Chapter 53

Building a Global Community

Many people mistakenly believe that monasteries were isolated prayer centers, but this is far from the truth. Benedictine monasteries were the social backbone of the Middle

Ages. Monasteries fed Europe, educated its leaders, produced tools and clothing, fostered trade, supplied social services, built churches, and ministered to the masses. Benedict's Rule hospitality requirements fostered a network for travelers that spawned trade and information exchanges. The Benedictine community went far beyond the cloister, and indeed encompassed the entire world.

The Benedictine global community was an early concept, dating from the first-generation Benedictine Pope Gregory the Great. Gregory used the economic surplus of the monasteries to feed a starving Italy and to fend off barbarian attacks. More importantly, he developed a hierarchical structure by which abbots reported to local bishops and,

NEW LANARK—SOCIAL PROFITABILITY

In the late 1800s, a glorious community-manufacturing center was developed in New Lanark, Scotland. The managerial pioneer Robert Owens built this highly profitable endeavor. Owens supplied two-room homes, garbage collection, and free education to his workforce. This was an experiment not in social philanthropy but in the importance of global community. His production of wood equaled that of the earlier great Benedictine communities. Robert

ultimately, to Rome. This assured a link to a larger community. It also allowed economic trade and growth, which was a positive factor for the individual monasteries. The Benedictine approach was to search for cooperative advantage between organizations and people.

Cooperative advantage is a principle similar to the idea of Benedictine communal welfare, where individual needs and organizational goals are mutually balanced. The Benedictine principle of cooperative advantage balances needs and goals between organizations. Benedictine monasteries supplied work, capital, and food to a social community that contributed labor and an economic market for the monastery. Consider Microsoft's partnership with the American

Owens theorized that investing in "living machinery" gives returns over 60 percent as opposed to the 15 percent realized from machines. The Owens model was a highly successful application of Benedictine principles in the Industrial Revolution. Owens also saw the total system of the working community as being global in nature. Owens broke other ground by employing children for only 10¾ hours a day without punishment. The Owens model became the basis for many of the religious pilgrims to the United States. New Lanark was also an industrial pioneer in the use of color and visual learning in his factories.   ❖

Library Association. Software, hardware, and technical expertise were donated to 1,000 libraries, thereby generating a new group of Microsoft users. Years ago, Apple donated computer labs to high schools, helping education but also developing a new generation of users. Charity can pay; in fact, the governing Rule of Benedictine monasteries was called *Perfecta Caritatis,* literally the "Charter of Charity." Benedictines realized early on that the success of the monastery depended on the local lay community.

Strategic Philanthropy

Microsoft and the American Library Association is an example of strategic philanthropy. Too many companies today view philanthropy as a one-way relationship. In turn, philanthropy is restricted to "must" situations, as when the Girl Scout shows up with her cookies. Strategic philanthropy is a pro-action search for a social partner. For example, research grants could be channeled to universities to address company problem-solving issues and continuous improvement. Many companies have utilized disabled workers for routine jobs. Strategic philanthropy is not less philanthropic, but it is more focused on a common destiny. Since the 1960s, Boeing has helped Pioneer Human Services provide jobs for recovering substance abusers and ex-offenders. The partnership supplies Boeing high quality components at a reasonable price. Pioneer has increased its revenues to forty million dollars and has put thousands to work.

Global Communal Welfare

Kaoru Ishikawa in his 1980 book *What Is Total Quality Control* highlighted an American weakness. From the Japanese perspective (one I believe to be correct), American industry does not look at the overall value to society in decision making. I can give a common example from my own automotive experience that shows this lack of a global view. In the forging bar industry, it was common for General Motors to ask for continually tighter tolerances (plus/minus allowances on bar diameters). The tighter tolerances were required to improve the quality of the steel suppliers. The banner became "half tolerance," meaning half the allowable range specified by the American Standards for Testing and Materials (ASTM). General Motors forced the steel forging industry into a competitive spiral to supply "half tolerance." Certainly half tolerance can be considered better engineered steel, but it came at a high price of investment and time by the steel manufacturers, which General Motors did not compensate. The real issue, however, was that General Motor's forging operations were not of significant technology to utilize the benefit of "half tolerance." The end forging, therefore, realized no significant quality improvement. The result was a dollar loss to society as a whole. General Motors caused a similar problem for flat roll steel companies when it went to Just-in-Time deliveries. Since the suppliers could not develop systems overnight, they were forced to keep sufficient inventory to supply on time, thus pushing up costs.

Cooperative Advantage

The Benedictine approach is always based on sharing, and that includes profits and advantages. The Benedictine monasteries also cooperated with the lay community for overall economic advantage. Crafts, in particular, were managed as a partnership. In agriculture, a joint venture approach

OLIVER SHELDON—A BENEDICTINE MANAGERIAL PHILOSOPHER

In his 1923 book *The Philosophy of Management* Sheldon looked at the broader scope of management and community. Sheldon was part of the social awakening in British industry. His novel approach put the human element above methods of production. His book set "rules" for management, six of which could have been written by St. Benedict:

- Workers should decide on the working conditions.
- Workers should receive a "civilized" standard of

known as granges was developed in cases where the local community lacked resources and skills. An interlocking network of organizations which today we might call a supply chain arose because of this. The strength of this network was its cooperative sharing and manufacturing. This is a model we use today in a society that is geared for social Darwinism (survival of the fittest). The Benedictine approach was to build a cooperative network, sharing gains and cooperating for the overall good of the network.

This type of cooperative network may require grain producers to supply at an "economic loss" so that the shepherds might gain an "economic advantage." The goal is

- Workers should receive a "civilized" standard of living
- Workers have leisure time for self-development
- Security from unemployment
- A share in industrial prosperity
- Spirit of equity

Sheldon works from the basis for many behavioral studies in management as well such techniques as gainsharing. Sheldon's novel approach continues to find more applications even today. In reading Sheldon, one can easily envision the hand of St. Benedict's Rule. Sheldon even suggested ties with the religious communication and government welfare agencies. ❖

similar to the Japanese view in business of the "good of society." Of course, this is a difficult application unless one can count on help coming both ways.

The application of Benedictine supply chain management and cooperative advantage requires a global view. The Japanese have this basic view. The cooperative advantage model is difficult to implement in a society based on competition. Our laws in particular restrict cooperation, because we believe that competitive advantage is the superior philosophy. Sharing even basic knowledge between companies can fall under anti-trust laws. The advance of basic knowledge should be communal. The Benedictine success shows that sharing basic knowledge will lead to more competition.

Applications of the Rule

I. CUSTOMER TEAMS/SUPPLIER PARTNERSHIPS

The sacrifices needed to achieve an overall economic benefit for society require partnerships. Suppliers and customers must come to know each other and work together. Ultimately community must be built, and this requires employee interaction. The use of supplier/customer teams is gaining acceptance today. In the long run, these teams cut costs for both partners. These teams tend to eliminate the finger pointing that is so common in supplier/customer relationships. The secret to these teams is that they must meet regularly (preferably over lunch!) in both good and bad times. Remember that the goal is to build community, and that requires social interactions between companies and employees. Supply partnerships need to aim for the Benedictine use of a partnership charter. The need is to interlock supply chain management into a common destiny.

2. INVOLVE EMPLOYEES IN YOUR STRATEGIC PHILANTHROPY

The term "global community" refers broadly to an organization interlinked with local communities. A strategic Benedictine approach necessitates a system view and total employee involvement. Companies miss opportunities if they do not involve their employees in the selection and distribution of corporate charities. Some companies, of course, have matching donations, which is excellent. Other opportunities are to send employee representatives rather than the CEO to dinners, banquets, and the like with gifts of charity. If you have a selection process for charities, involve all levels of employees in it. Employee involvement will forge the links to bind communities together.

10

Building and Implementing a Benedictine Organization

A Senior chosen for skill in winning souls should be appointed to look after the newcomer with careful attention.

—Benedict's Rule, Chapter 58

Do not grant newcomers to the monastic life an easy entry, but, as the apostle says, "Test the spirits to see if they are from God."

—Benedict's Rule, Chapter 58

The reason we have written this rule is that, by observing it in monasteries, we can show

*that we have some degrees of virtue and
the beginnings of monastic life. But for everyone hastening on to the perfection of
monastic life, there are the teachings of
early church writers.*

—Benedict's Rule, Chapter 73

Developing a Rule

The keystone of a Benedictine organization is an organizational Rule. A Rule is much more than a mission statement; it is an employee handbook. Benedict's Rule would be a pamphlet or small pocket book in length, yet it is enough to bring meaning to the mission. Mission and vision statements cover many walls, but rarely have organizational impact. A Rule, on the other hand, explains mission and incorporates it into action within the organization. A Rule is to be studied, understood, and discussed. A Rule is a starting point for new managers and employees. In a Benedictine monastery, a section of the Rule was read and discussed each morning in chapter. That type of emphasis is needed in organizations to bring mission statements to life. Benedict's Rule was written in a manner that was self-promoting.

There may be some hesitation at implementing a system that has a monastic background, but many organizations have been highly successful with parts of this model. IBM's high technology longevity is rooted in its rules and culture;

it even has a corporate songbook. Universities are examples of the Benedictine employee selection and leadership principles. Cooperative advantage is growing in all industries. Gainsharing plans are popular in many industries. Written missions and procedures are gaining popularity with the advent of ISO 9000. The Benedictine model offers the risk-taker even greater rewards. Leadership selection is one of those areas where new ground can be broken.

There are even examples of well-written corporate rules. One of the best was written for the nuclear industry and is called *Excellence in Human Performance*. This is an outstanding manual written by working groups including utility operators, craft personnel, supervisors, and managers, as well as personnel from other industries. The focus is on a trial of overriding principles:

1. Organizational Processes and Values (includes creating a learning environment;
2. Individual Behaviors; and
3. Leader Behaviors

This thirty-two-page pocket book is a Benedictine ideal.

Benedict's genius was his understanding of the breakdown of the Roman system. His cybernetic design of the Rule required training and on-going discussion of the Rule. This type of internal design allowed it to be applied for fifteen hundred years, a record unmatched by any other organization or government. The power of the Rule is its length—it is long enough to explain and guide, but is still short of being a bible or canon of laws. It limited the number of "laws" to a handful, giving authority to management to rule. The Rule has three levels of documentation—mission, core principles, and procedures. Developing a Rule can be done with a few steps and a lot of employee input.

STEP 1: IDENTIFY AND DESCRIBE THE CORE PRINCIPLES OF YOUR ORGANIZATION

Benedict's Rule never really presents a mission statement, but rather elaborates on a set of core principles including Christian belief, obedience, and humility. These core principles are then explained and justified as the basis of the organization. Benedict does this in his longest section of the Rule, the Prologue. Many followers have argued that Benedict really had a very brief mission—*Laborare Est Orare*—to work is to pray. I believe a very brief mission statement (two sentences maximum) could be a cover page. The use of a short Latin phrase such as the *semper fiedlis* of the marines is good also. The mental translation requires thinking rather than passive acceptance. Step 1 is a top-down process. Core principles must come before organization since they are its pillars. Top management must define core principles.

STEP 2: DEFINE AND EXPLAIN YOUR CULTURE

Benedict's Chapter 1 (a chapter in the Rule is about half a page or less of text) presents a comparison of monastic types to rationalize his approach known as cenobites. He explains differences and sets up what the Rule expects culturally. This is important in any rule, because it allows the new employee to integrate into the organization more efficiently. A software specialist would find extremely different cultures at Apple and IBM. A Rule can even help for a better mutual employment decision. An IBM software manager would be out of place in the freewheeling style of Apple. Better to realize this during the initial interview. Culture shows support for core principles and vice versa. Step 2 is the middle management process. Culture must be built by middle management. It is middle management where the vision of the top meets the reality of the workforce.

STEP 3: BUILD PROCEDURES AND ORGANIZATION TO SUPPORT MISSION AND CULTURE

Benedict's Rule is loaded with supporting procedures. These procedures cover selection of managers, daily routine, discipline, position requirements, community rank, meal times, etc. Procedures must be built from the bottom up based on the mission, core principles, and culture or the organization. All employees should be involved in writing procedures. For this to be effective, there must be training on the core principles. Procedures should have a supporting role, and not break new ground.

The real problem today with procedures is that they lack Benedictine brevity and focus. Benedictine procedures are guides to employees; they are not work instructions. In the Benedictine organization, training passes work instructions. In my consulting for the implementation of ISO 9000 in industry, I found that most of the waste and cost is in writing endless, never-followed work instructions where a Benedictine procedure would suffice. A Benedictine procedure has a simple format answering who, when, what, and how. The procedure itself should never be longer than a paragraph. A paragraph procedure assures it to be an operating guide that directs rather than instructs. Instruction should be dealt with in training. If work instructions are needed, they should be put in a training manual. Benedictine monks were not robots, they were guided, and trusted, participants.

Another thing that must be avoided is a document that requires constant change. The focus should be on a level where change is not common. Detailed procedures and work instructions have no place in an organization because, by their nature, they change with the environment. This idea should help in the writing of a corporate Rule. Procedures dependent on equipment, specific customers, and specific products are outside the scope of a corporate Rule. When making the decision on whether to include something in your corporate Rule (employee manual), ask if it will need updating in the next five years. This may be the hardest question in the writing of your employee manual (Rule). Yet, stability of Benedict's Rule is at the heart of organizational stability. Employee manuals that frequently change reflect a high level of entropy (disorder). The development of this manual should help you focus on the very foundation of your organization.

A manual written in stone is foreign to most of us. We must remember Benedict's concept of built-in flexibility. The Rule sets discipline but allows leaders to be flexible in application. The strength of the Rule is its built-in ability to change while still remaining rigid (*Mobili in Mobilis*). This indeed is the essence of good management. It is this type of management that makes the difference between empowerment and anarchy. The problem Benedict saw in Roman rules was their lack of cybernetics. Rigidity is needed for stability but there must be a built-in steering mechanism for natural change since change itself is a constant.

STEP 4: TRAIN ON THE RULE

Once your Rule is in manual form, it should be a training tool. The Rule must be the focus of all training—from it all training flows. Therefore, all training should be prefixed by its relationship to the corporate mission. Employees should be looking for a link to the corporate manual. The manual should be on-the-job training and a well-used reference. This brings us to a key point. A Benedictine leader leads by example, leaders therefore must be well versed in the manual. Furthermore, the leader must be consistent with the Rule.

As part of the training, the Benedictine approach uses the mentor system. The mentor system has a dual function in that it gives a key role to senior employees while developing new employees. Mentor training programs need to be formal. Too often employees are left on their own to develop, which often results in the emergence of a counter culture. A mentor develops loyalty and obedience in the new employee as well as culture.

STEP 5: DESIGN CLOSURE ON INITIAL TRAINING OF YOUR RULE

Training (classroom, mentor, and on-the-job) should be for a specific period. Six months to a year should be about right. This initiation period must end in acceptance of the corporate rule and culture. The end of the first year is the time to discuss the future with new employees. At this point, a commitment on both sides is needed. Also, there should be an "initiation" or graduation party to welcome the new member to the community.

Actually the Rule of Benedict has a three-phase initiation period. After the first two months, the Rule was read and the monks were told, "This is the law under which you are choosing to serve. If you can keep it, come in. If not, feel free to leave." This commitment was requested again in six months, and finally, in the tenth month. The Rule asked for acceptance, not submission. This approach eliminates negativity and forms *esprit de corps* early on. Remember that the Rule is not a union contract; it is guide to a common destiny.

STEP 6: CONTINUOUS TRAINING AND IMPROVEMENT
Benedict was truly an organizational visionary; his last chapter would fit textbooks today. Benedict sees his Rule as merely a start on the journey to excellence. Continuous improvement is a part of the Rule. Benedict talks of going to other resources beyond the Rule.

Employee Selection

Employee selection is key to building an effective Benedictine organization. The longevity of Benedictine organizations is based on employee selection, training, and buy-in (initiation). Selection is based on virtues such as obedience and humility. Benedictine organizations like to hire virgins with no experience except education and move them up the organization. Selection must be mutual. The corporate Rule and culture must be carefully laid out in the initial exchange. Microsoft is a big believer in the virgin approach because it is easier to build culture. The Benedictine approach, however, does not limit itself to virgins. The key is the willingness to adapt to a new culture. Actually, Benedict was highly selective. He commonly rejected potential members to test their desire.

This approach is common to organizations such as the

Marines, IBM, Microsoft, top universities, specific fraternities, and the like. These organizations do not adjust their
selection criteria in poor times or because of a changing environment. These organizations are internally stable and
culturally strong. This strength and stability becomes an at-
traction in itself. A Benedictine organization is built for the
long run. In the 1970s great counterculture revolution,
many were predicting an end of the University of Michi-
gan's forty-plus fraternities. It was true that many of those
did fail. Amazingly, those that failed were those that tried
the hardest to adapt to the new culture. The traditional con-
servative fraternities suffered at times during leaner years
but ultimately survived as organizations. IBM, with all its
mistakes over the last thirty years, survives because of its
organizational infrastructure (Rule and culture). This is exactly how Benedict saw organizational survival fifteen
hundred years ago. The oldest single organization, the
Catholic Church (fifteen hundred years old) was a result of
Gregory the Great applying the Benedictine Rule to the
church organization.

"The barbarians learned agriculture from the monks.
In fact, it was monks that brought sheep farming in
medieval England and taught the populace weaving,
the wool trade becoming the foundation of the national economy."—Julian Stead, *St. Benedict: A
Rule for Beginners*

Implementation

Benedictine principles are part common sense and part understanding of human nature. Any organization can improve productivity and efficiency from their application. Some of the principles are part of the new movement toward process control and procedure documentation such as ISO 9000. Other principles are counterculture today. Benedict's employee empowerment, for example, is unique. Benedict allowed for hierarchical structure and supervision while maximizing empowerment by leadership selection. Empowering employees more in leadership selection does present a challenge. Still, considering some of the almost bizarre Japanese techniques that were implemented in the 1980s, Benedictine principles are more evolutionary than revolutionary. Leadership selection is merely the ultimate in employee empowerment.

Benedict's total system approach is very consistent with the popular Deming principles. The development of a Rule is consistent with the Baldridge Total Management approach to operations. The suggestions and steps laid out in this study of Benedictine principles can be brought in slowly. Benedictine principles are soundly rooted in our culture. Western government, military, and churches all have deep Benedictine roots.

Appendix

Chapter Headings in Benedict's Rule

Chapter 1   The different kinds of monks and their customs

Chapter 2   The qualities of the abbot

Chapter 3   The counsel of the brothers

Chapter 4   The instruments of good works

Chapter 5   Obedience

Chapter 6   Silence

Chapter 7   Humility

Chapter 8   The Divine Office at night (Matins)

Chapter 9   How many psalms are to be said in the Night Office

Chapter 10   How the Night Office is to be said in summer

Chapter 11   How Matins is to be celebrated on Sundays

Chapter 12   Lauds—celebration

Chapter 13   Lauds—ordinary days

Chapter 14   Night Office on Saints Days

The Benedictine Reader

About the Rule

Chittister, Joan. *The Rule of Benedict: Insights for the Ages.* New York: Crossroad, 1992.

Meisel, Anthony, and M. L. Del Mastro. *The Rule of Saint Benedict.* Garden City, N.Y.: Image Books, 1975.

Stead, Julian. *Saint Benedict: A Rule for Beginners.* New Rochelle, N.Y.: New City Press, 1993.

Benedictine Concepts

Davis, Gordon, and Scott Hamilton. *Managing Information: How Information Systems Impact Organizational Strategy.* Homewood, Ill: Business One Irwin, 1993.

Dessler, Gary. *Winning Commitment: How to Build and Keep a Competitive Workforce.* New York: McGraw-Hill, 1993.

Kouzes, James, and Barry Posner. *The Leadership Challenge: How to Keep Getting Extraordinary Things Done in Organizations.* San Francisco, C.A.: Jossey-Bass Publishers, 1995.

Miyamoto, Musashi. *A Book of Five Rings*. Trans. Victor Harris. Woodstock, N.Y.: Overlook Press, 1974, 1982.

Reich, Robert. *The Future of Success: Working and Living in the New Economy*. New York: Alfred A. Knopf, 2001.

Senge, Peter. *The Fifth Discipline: The Art and Practice of the Learning Organization*. New York: Doubleday, 1994.

Smith, Hedrick. *Rethinking America*. New York: New York: Random House, 1995.

Sun Tzu [Sunzi]. *The Art of War*. Trans. Thomas Cleary. Boston, M.A.: Shambhala, 1988.

Waitley, Denis. *Empires of the Mind: Lessons to Lead and Succeed in a Knowledge-Based World*. New York: William Morrow and Company, 1995.